Arabs

Arabs

Mark Allen

continuum

CONTINUUM

The Tower Building, 11 York Road, London SE1 7NX
80 Maiden Lane, Suite 704, New York, NY 10038

www.continuumbooks.com

First published 2006
Reprinted 2006 (three times)
First published in paperback 2007

British Library Cataloguing-in-Publication Data
A catalogue record for this book is available from the British Library.

ISBN 978 0 8264 9055 1 (hb)
ISBN 978 0 8264 9402 3 (pb)

Typeset by YHT Ltd, London
Printed and bound by MPG Books Ltd, Bodmin, Cornwall

Contents

Introduction   1

 1 In Search of the Arabs   3
 2 Blood   11
 3 Religion   25
 4 Community   43
 5 Women   59
 6 The Problem of Power   72
 7 Politics   86
 8 Modernity   101
 9 Language and Signals   118
10 Outlook   131

Bibliography   143

Introduction

I came to Arabic and the world of the Arabs by chance. In 1970, I wanted to change my course at Oxford from Classics to Turkish and was told that I could only do this if I chose Arabic as my main subject. I had a hard year with classical Arabic before I visited the Lebanon, Syria and Egypt. I had been a falconer since I was 14 and I had already started Arabic before I discovered that some Arabs also love falconry. That helped. It was 34 years before I got back to Turkey.

After Oxford, I spent a year living in Jordan. I had a light teaching job in Amman and a team of hawks. I bought a thoroughbred camel and together we explored the eastern parts of Jordan. I spent as much time as I could with my falconer friends. Few of them spoke any English.

Returning to London, I joined the Foreign Service and, after further Arabic training in the Lebanon, I served in our embassies in Abu Dhabi and Cairo. From 1981 I had a break from the Arab world. I was posted to Belgrade for four years and later dealt with Eastern European affairs in London. In 1990, just in time for the Iraqi invasion of Kuwait, I returned to serve in Amman for four years. Thereafter, until I retired in 2004, my work in London took me all over the world, but often to the Middle East. I visited Arab countries frequently. The only ones I have not seen are Tunisia and the Yemen.

In this book I try to draw out the unmistakable character formed by a distinctive culture. The Arabs, for all their geographical and historical variety, have a powerful personality. It comes of a deeply held respect for the individual and for the moral ideas which define the person in community. Four main themes are visible in this

1

attitude – family, religion, Arabism and power. These, I believe, are important across the Arab world and allow us the possibility of speaking, as the Arabs do, about the Arabs in general.

Arabism is the mission of being self-consciously true to the Arab identity and the sense of it has run, now strong and insistent, now weak, throughout the Arabs' long story. I call it aspirational because, even for Arabs in Arabia who can hardly be called anything other than Arab, this sense seems also to be of an ideal to which the individual feels he or she must aspire. The political history of the Arabs, so entwined with family, religion and Arabism, has given the Arabs a quite different direction of development from our own. Power – who wields it, who should wield it and why – has always been a core theme. Power is now in dispute and the dispute about it is causing uneasiness both inside the Arab world and for the rest of us outside it.

I am often asked about the Arab world and have written for those who are not closely involved in it. Those who are and, of course, the Arabs themselves will assert their own points of view. My view is simply my own, grown and tested across the years. Its mistakes are my own and not those of my friends. I have avoided names in this book. Those who read it and see their influence in it will know how much I owe them.

Chapter 1

In search of the Arabs

'It is the person that matters.'   St Teresa of Avila

This book is about Arabs – Arabs as people and what has made them the way they are. The level of noise about the Arabs has been steadily rising. In the past 15 years, outsiders have twice sent armies to war in the Middle East – to liberate Kuwait from Saddam and then to overthrow him in Iraq. Chronic strife has also afflicted Algeria, the Sudan, the Lebanon and by extension Syria. Palestinians and Israelis have seen long periods of violence. Specialists have been watching with alarm the way radical Islamism[1] has been mutating into some kind of new armed struggle. The disaster of 11 September 2001 precipitated 'The War on Terror'. Scarcely an Arab country has been free of terrorist attacks or the tension of retaliatory operations against terrorist groups. Saudi Arabia and Iraq have faced unprecedented internal security difficulties. The Middle East contains two-thirds of proven oil reserves and the price of oil has been climbing. Advisers working on security assessments for foreigners in the region have blanched.

Futurologists forecast that if European populations are to maintain today's proportions of workers to pensioners, tens of millions of migrants will be needed and many of these are expected to come to Europe from Arab countries. Yet a rising level of general migration, a sub-trend of globalization, has already made immigration a hot

---

1 Islamism/Islamists: these are the usual terms now for what we once inaccurately used to call 'fundamentalism/fundamentalists'. Islamists are those who seek to impose a radically conservative vision of Islam as a political programme for society. Their vision (see Chapters 3 and 8) concentrates on the achievements of the early Islamic community, as interpreted by an ancient puritanical tradition.

issue in European politics. Around the world, worry about the proliferation of weapons of mass destruction, particularly the danger of their possible use by terrorists, underlies a new and more general concern about conditions in the Middle East. In many democracies, the terrorist threat is prompting a new debate about what security measures can be adopted and at what cost to important freedoms. The sense of impending turbulence in some Arab countries has provoked a new and more searching look at these countries' political arrangements. Is there a link, people are asking, between inflexible politics in the region and the growing diaspora of violence and dissent? The outsiders' guess is that not enough freedom in the Middle East may be at the root of the trouble.

So the noise of events is being amplified by comment, debate and attitude. Even a patient person might ask why another book on all this? We are confused enough by an overload of information. It feels like Babel – an address in Iraq, once a metaphor for the impracticality of ambition, and also the title of one of the Ba'thist regime's daily newspapers. A surfeit of analyses would be a heavy cure. We know the headlines we read and the unremitting emphasis on violence. Yet few of us seem to have much to say about the Arab as person – someone to meet, with whom to do business, or with whom to co-exist in a globalizing world as a neighbour. My book looks at what defines the Arab as a person, the influences and conditions which tell us what the Arab is like and, perhaps, why. This is not a history book, a narrative, though it has to take due account of the past of a people for whom the past is so important.

An ornithologist would say that I am interested in the jizz of the Arab. This is his jargon for the overall and essential impression a bird makes. The bird's characteristics, like the teeth of a Yale key, lift the levers of recognition. The jizz is almost the spirit of the thing, an unmistakable and telling communication of self. 'It's me ... ' and 'Yes, of course,' we reply, 'it's you – who else?' The subliminal, hook-and-eye match up, no matter how hard to define or articulate, is convincing and very often accurate. The compound which makes up this key which unlocks an identity from the memory in a flash of recognition, is the jizz.

Arabs have jizz, big jizz. The question is what are its elements? What are those characteristics which put a smile of familiarity on our faces, which illuminate a hinterland of other likely characteristics which may not yet have been visible? And this is not a matter of ethnography or precepts to which individuals ought to conform, but simply the deposit of experience, how it turns out to be over these many long years of watching, listening and being both friends and enemies.

One of the more acute critiques of the Arab world is that there is a deficit of institutions. Institutions are our way of protecting ourselves from personalities and the human factor in the abuse of power. In the West, we now have so many institutions that today we concentrate on their internal workings, hence the new theologies of 'Process is Substance' and 'Transparency'. In the Arab world, the picture is not the same and that troubles us. The deficit, we wonder, may be part of the reason for the apparent instabilities and disturbance. This, however, too easily obscures something else which is just as interesting.

The striking characteristic of the Arab world is that it is personal. There, and for them, persons matter most. The whole culture and social order of the Arab world is built around persons in community, not collectives of people without names. For this reason, institutions (which do of course exist in some ways) are not the point and indeed they pose awkward contradictions for societies built around people, household and family, rather than dynasty and prince. We know about the personal nature of power in the Middle East and criticize it, but we also need a wider look to understand what changes may be really acceptable to the people there and likely to engage their loyalty.

For amid the noise and general concern, a further and subtle danger approaches and that is our own vulnerability to seeking comfort and refuge in polarizing ourselves and a problem. Our own desire for ethical probity excites this binary assessment. 'I am here and you are over there; I am good and threatened; you are threatening and must be bad.' This tendency of ours to polarize often makes the other a two-dimensional and anonymous object. We lose track of the personal.

Arabs, to be sure, are controversial. Their culture and psychology have strong personality and it is not to everyone's taste. Their political story is turbulent and, as I write, whether they like it or not, they are widely associated with a new order of violence in the world. This violence is also directed against us by Islamist radicals and many of these are Arabs. One could argue that the book to write would be a slamming attack on their world and the background which brought these terrorists to the fore. Knocking copy would surely sell well. Many are alarmed by what they hear from the Middle East and our fear stirs hostility. Linda Blandford's *Oil Sheikhs*, which sent up the Gulf Arabs, did very well in 1976. It was written a couple of years after the oil embargo. David Pryce-Jones's *The Closed Circle*,[2] a polemic written from the point of view of Zionist sympathies, caught a public demand for bad news in 1989. Conversely, a book of mine about falconry in Arabia which came out in 1980 scarcely got going in the United States. An American told my publisher that, so soon after the siege of the American Embassy in Tehran in 1979, 'Turbans are out.'

I remember once being asked in quite an important interview which had strayed onto my interest in the Middle East, whether I would like to be an Arab. I was astonished. The thought had never occurred to me. I reflected that the closest I had ever got to this idea was in consoling myself, in times of stress or war, that I, unlike the Arabs, could get away home at the end of it. The question was put to me by someone who presented himself as a psychologist. It was a conventional tack and seemed to express a common assumption. This is that just as Arabs are controversial and unsympathetic to many people, they nonetheless exercise a powerful influence over those who get to know them, a romantic magnetism which pulls us away from our own roots and sets us up on alien barricades in foreign places. T. E. Lawrence is the conventional example.[3] Walter

2 London, Weidenfeld & Nicolson, 1989.

3 Lawrence crisply set out his own views on working with the Arab army in the Arab Revolt in his article, 'Twenty-Seven Articles', *Arab Bulletin*, 20 August 1917. It is reprinted in *Secret Despatches from Arabia*, ed. Malcolm Brown (London, Bellew Publishing, 1991).

de la Mare hinted at the same in his poem 'Arabia', 'He is crazed with the spell of far Arabia / They have stolen his wits away.'

The assumption is primitive. Those who have lived among the Arabs discover that granite hard-headedness coexists with romantic sensibilities in about the same proportions as we find, say, in Scotland. The paradox is vivid and defies explanation. In thinking about this book, paradox is a word I find often recurring. Paradox is untidy, but an assurance of the human. Meanness and generosity, violence and gentleness, formality and sympathy, pragmatism and idealism, nostalgia and realism – these are some of the contradictions which keep one awake in the Arabian night, wondering how to make sense of what is at once so familiar and human, yet so deeply foreign. A slamming book would not capture the paradox which is itself part of the jizz.

It is true that we can be misled by the personal, but this is certainly not just the *déformation professionel* of the expert on the spot. How many important outsiders have come back from visits to the Middle East, convinced that they have a personal understanding with some powerful figure, if not a personal undertaking from him? The conviction lasts simply about as long as the visitor's patience, once home again and waiting for the outcome. The idiom is our own. We think of the personal as implying some sincerity. We do not like to think that, in our dealings with others, a number of things may be going on at the same time. Or, at least, if we do, then it is a broader sweep of considerations proper to our own side, and not the other's. The cold professional and the sere official are familiar figures from our tradition of blocs, systems, apparats and institutions. In the Arab world, the personal is just closer to the surface than it is in our own. And the personal brings us close to culture, the first formatting of personality by the group.

For us, the effort to take all this in is great. The standards expected of relationships there are high and we have to put a good deal of ourselves into the effort, to measure up. In casual contact with Arabs, this point is not always clear and so we overlook it. When disappointed, we detach. Relations suffer and so do the possibilities for finding workable ways through the problems we face.

The great modern account of Arab history is Albert Hourani's *A History of the Arab Peoples.*[4] Hourani was careful to touch in his title on the diversity of the Arabs – there is no 'one size fits all'. The significance of Arab identity and its components have shifted, ebbed and flowed across the centuries. When Hourani was finishing his book in the early 1990s, it seemed that we were reaching a phase of greater diversity, a less self-conscious commitment to Arabism of the kind we had seen earlier in the century with Arab nationalists, like Nasser. So the answers to 'Who is an Arab?' are untidy and have meant different things at different points in history.

There is an aspirational approach to 'Arab-ness', being an Arab, and it lies, I believe, near the heart of the Arab jizz. There are people who count themselves Arab, but who have never lived in the Arab world and do not speak Arabic. There are people who consider themselves Arabs, but who have (as do, for instance, the descendants of African slaves) antecedents who had little or no connection with the Arab world. For them, the pull is very great; and within the wide Arab community stands an awareness that being Arab means to some extent also measuring up, measuring up to the great models of Islamic and Arab history and also to the moral ideals which have made the Arab so distinctive from earliest times. The aspiration is both individual and collective for the Arabs are supremely gregarious. And, across all their diversities, their common language supplies the means to communicate and hear these shared values.

Freddy Beeston, who was the Professor of Arabic at Oxford, once told a junior colleague that if he had an idea for a book, he would do well to put it by for 30 years – then he would write a better book. I have tried to follow his advice but, in consequence, have not written the book I first intended. I wanted to bring out the personal and thought to do that through the free use of examples and personalities. I found Arabic at Oxford very difficult and I do not suppose I ever really learned how to speak it. Instead, countless generous and hospitable Arabs kindly talked me into it. Thirty-five years later their memory and friendship remain vivid. But the years have also

4 Hourani, Albert, *A History of the Arab Peoples* (London, Faber, 1993).

brought affairs in the Arab world to such a pass that it would be no return of friendship to speak of individuals. Political sensitivities are set on a hair-trigger. And, as Lawrence noted in 1917,[5] we are never as popular in Arabia as we may like to think. Furthermore, a gregarious people have a strong culture and strong cultures have strong boundaries. My belief in the importance of giving greater depth to our sense of the Arabs will give little pleasure to them – they stand on their own strong identity and defend their boundaries. Their world is personal and so also, in our categories of thought, private. They do not welcome observation and are quick to spot what, in their own terms, seems a mistaken view or understanding. They will find plenty to fault, from all angles according to geography and prejudice, in what I have to say, in this effort to look inside.

The years have also given me the chance to draw from the uniqueness of individual personalities, themes which I now see amount to a powerful jizz. As can be seen from the chapter headings, these themes, always shifting, coalescing and separating across the centuries, are the Arabs' context and their aspirations: family, religion, the Arab identity held in common, and the collective experience of power. These affect the individual's sense of being a social person and his language. I see the situation of women in the Arab world as almost a metaphor for the situation of society in the face of power and so they have their own chapter. The response to modernity tells us much about the Arab past and the fundamental nature of much we might otherwise reckon is incidental.

Some readers may feel a narrowness in my account, a concentration on some abstracted notion of the Arab who often appears to be tribal. Some may feel this because their own experience of the Arabs has not given them much contact with the Arabian. The Arabian is not familiar and they may want to say that their experience of the Arabs has all seemed quite different. Their friends in the Beirut restaurant or the office block in Cairo do not conform to what seem period stereotypes. I know how foreign and unwelcome the tribal scene still remains in its wider context of today's

5 See Lawrence's paper above at note 3.

9

Arab society, both in terms of strong social prejudice and political sensitivity. Nonetheless, the Arabs themselves propose themselves as a collective and in looking at its features it is inescapable that Arabia remains the taproot of Arab identity and the source of its strength, no matter how much things changed when non-Arab influences from the north, Byzantines, Persians, Turks and Europeans started to get their hands on the new centres of power. This background clearly has some reality. It deserves and needs inclusion. For those of us who are not Arabs, it is primary material for understanding the sophistications of today's more variegated world

My object is to get clear the elemental values and influences which, whether or not ascribed by individuals to an Arabian past, do weigh distinctively on the men and women of today in the Arab world. And the extent to which the origin of these values and influences may not be recognized may be the extent to which other influences have combined with the core themes. We speak of the rule of the 'Abbasid caliphs in mediaeval Baghdad as 'the Arab empire', but it was scarcely Arab from many points of view. It wanted, however, to be Arab. So it had to look not only back, but also affirm for today and tomorrow the heritage of that past. Today, that same yen is expressed in the language of a religious commitment to a revelation. That revelation was revealed in Arabic and first to the Arabs of Arabia.

Family, religion, Arabism and the collective experience of power reveal what is personal to every Arab. I believe we shall make more sense of the 250 million Arabs who live just across the Mediterranean if we recognize what is important and of value to them.

Chapter 2

Blood

Blood is a sign of lineage and purity, a sign of life itself. It is a dense idea and strange to our own experience. For the Arab peoples of the Middle East, blood is elemental to their value system and daily lives. They take blood very seriously. For them, blood is the assurance of identity and family, the premise on which a vigorous honour code is built and a framework of social organization exists which acts as a metaphor for other groupings beyond strict connections of kinship. Blood ties define personal interests and beliefs; blood, therefore, has a direct impact on the moral life. At the extreme, the blood feud, for instance, can put personal identity and obligation to dramatic test, and the need to support weaker or older members of the family can incur real personal sacrifice. We see it thus, but the imperatives of family solidarity can also be opportunities to affirm identity and values. In asking who the Arabs are and what are they like, there seems no escape from an answer that begins with blood.

In the book of Genesis, the archangel Gabriel tells Abraham that God will bless him and make his descendants as numerous as the stars of the heaven, as the sand on the sea shore. In Abraham's seed all the nations of the earth will be blessed because he obeyed God's voice and was ready to offer his son Isaac as a sacrifice.[1]

The scene is familiar to us – we may have known it since early childhood when we were taught the Old Testament stories. We accept the odd diction of the angel: this is a story from a distant place at the beginning of time. We scarcely dwell on how such a conversation would strike us, were the angel speaking to us today,

1 Genesis 22.17–18.

11

now, in this room. And so we miss this glimpse of a mentality and an outlook which are so radically different from our own.

I asked a shaikh from a large tribe in Arabia what he thought about blood. He strongly insisted that blood mattered before everything else. I suggested that this was a view shared with the other Semites, and particularly the Jews. I mentioned the Bible story of Gabriel blessing Abraham. 'Look,' he said, 'Ibrahim was an Arab and he is our father. He did not come from New York, Poland or London. His son was Isma'il and he is our father.' Ibrahim is the Arabic for Abraham and his soubriquet, *al-Khalil*, means 'the Friend (of God)' – hence the Arabs' name for Hebron where Abraham is buried, is *al-Khalil*. The patriarch's sacrifice to God was in the blood of the ram. He stands in mind daily in the mention of God's name in the slaughter of animals.[2]

Ibrahim *al-Khalil*, Abraham, was not blessed in a way which might make sense to us – given some good fortune, some reward or prize that would enrich his life. He is told instead that his family will grow, be multiplied beyond counting or imagination. This to Abraham is a blessing indeed. With our different mentality and ideas about home budgeting, we might well sympathize with a friend who, in receipt of such a message from an angel, spoke of a moment's alarm, if not panic. For Abraham, however, the assurance of descendants into the unfathomable future is on the same spiritual dimension as an assurance of eternity.

One of the greatest paradoxes of the Arabian tribal ego is that profound gregariousness coexists with intense individuality. Thus identity is always frequency hopping between the wavelength of the 'I' and 'what I want' and other longer wavelengths of family and the demands of the wider group. On these longer wavelengths, the Arab is in contact with an almost transcendental awareness of the collective. Lineage rises behind him in great genealogies of forebears with peaks, like mountains, going up to Abraham, and, in front, the hope of descendants running before him like a river branching out

---

2 This mention of the name of God as the throat is slit makes the meat *halal* and thus permitted as food.

into a delta, spreading and diversifying until slipping into a wide and limitless sea. Abraham was moved by such a vision and it still resonates with the Arab of today.

Arab society is patrilineal. An Arab's second name is his or her father's. Fathers trace their line back to founders of tribes. Founders of tribes relate to ancestors whose patriarchal names put them among the descendants of Abraham. Women are not mentioned in these family trees (Arabs also speak of family trees). However, no one is fooled about the apparent insignificance of the women (a saying goes that two-thirds of the boy's character are his mother's brothers) even though the women are not listed. When getting to know a large Arab family, or tribe, if you understand the subliminal network provided by matrilineal relationships, you have the key to much behaviour that would otherwise be misunderstood. There have been exceptions to this patrilineal tradition – some of the famous pre-Islamic poets were named after their mothers – but the generalization holds both geographically across the Arab world and in time across Arab history.

A patrilineal society is not necessarily the prisoner of its past, but the past exerts strong influence. Age is respected and a certain nostalgia for a real or imagined heroic history in the collective past sets wide horizons of achievement imagery ahead for the ambitious young. Cicero gave his view that men only start their mature years at 40. An Arab's story definitely enters a new phase when he achieves a new seniority on the death of his father. The memories of fathers, grandfathers and ancestors are extolled and celebrated. Proverbs and poetry ruefully tell the truth that 'We do not build like our forebears built'. And this, to the subtle and quick Semitic mind, leaves a sure implication about the irreducible honour and prestige of today's members of the family. They emerge as the inheritors and expressions today of a grand tradition.

One of the terrorists who seized the aeroplanes on 11 September 2001 is reportedly remembered by those who were at primary school with him. 'He was always a bad lot. His mother was not from here.' This captures the aversion to the danger of outbreeding, of breaking the old preference for marrying the daughter of a father's brother. It also, subtly, conveys the implication that the father was a bad lot too – he could not get the agreement of an uncle to let him have a cousin to marry, or, for that matter, the girl's agreement either. For girls do, in fact, have the right, admittedly not always allowed, to put their foot down and refuse a proposal or an arranged marriage. Instead, the father took to a stranger at a disadvantage (because she was a guest worker in an oil-producing state) and, if he did so out of lust, then his error was doubled. Love matches between cousins and equals are fabled and always thought the best. Marrying for looks is not. I once tried to make a happy and inoffensive comment on the news that an Arab grandee's son had got engaged. I said, 'I am sure she is very beautiful and that they will be happy together.' I got a withering look from the father who actually prided himself on his Westernized culture, and the icy observation that in marriage, in the Arab world, looks were of no account. Blood is what matters; and even if attitudes are changing a little among the young, it will be generations before the deep instinct for family as history and future alters course. Blood ties provide the human context. It explains why in Arab society the personal is so much more prominent than the institutional.

Family, clan and tribe provide identity. Identity works not only objectively, a label for securing recognition in the lowest sense, but subjectively also in asserting a moral agenda of collective honour, individual dignity and therefore acceptance as a truly free person. Arabs who still consider themselves tribal look on those who do not maintain a tribal connection, like farmers, villagers and towns-people, as being not free. These detribalized people are believed not to know their origins and therefore their identity is qualified by uncertainty. They submit to the power of rulers, foreign or not. They have no purity or honour to defend. Whatever the prejudice here, the thought is advanced as a simple statement of fact. The blood-line has gone; the honour is compromised. Further down this supposed pecking order, in the village and town, of course the same assertion is made with conviction. 'Everybody knows where he is from, but not that family over there. They don't.' I asked a retired cabinet minister in Jordan about his story, meaning his own, and I knew he was a Palestinian. He began, in quite a matter of fact and casual way, 'My people hail from the Yemen ... ' As it turned out, this was some many centuries ago. His intention, in a country where the Palestinians are not considered 'top drawer' by the East Bank Jordanians, but where the founder of the state came from Mecca, was to demonstrate that he had as good a past as any and from deep in Arabia. Recent diversions and events could not erase that.

Arab society is patrilineal and where this is more obvious, as in Arabia, it is also segmentary. This anthropologist's term for a phenomenon which is not immediately obvious to us because we do not share the same social system, is captured in the Arab proverb, 'I against my cousin, my cousin and I against the stranger.' We can take this just as a sceptical assessment of the endemic difficulties to be found in large families and clans, or of the problems Arab governments have in joining forces for decisive action. In fact, it explains the practical operation of the Arabs' patrilineal system and how it aims to secure freedom and equality for each individual.

In the metaphor of the family tree, the individual is the leaf at the edge. He traces his line back along twig, branch, limb and trunk to get to the start of the tree which represents the founder of the tribe. Each join, as the individual traces backwards marks a generational shift. The cousins join up at the grandfather: the branch they have in common. And so on. In tribal practice, the basic unit which takes collective responsibility for matters of individual behaviour (e.g. killings), is the group descending from the same ancestor five generations back. Two individuals, if they count back from father to grandfather and meet the same forebear within five generations or less, are members of the same '*ahl*', a technical use of a term which usually and broadly means something like 'extended family'. This is the individual's vengeance group which is bound, if he is killed, to kill the killer or his close relatives in retaliation or raise a claim against them.

These groups form the main unit segments of the tribe. They develop in parallel and are therefore set in natural competition, a 'them and us' distinction which can be enlarged into greater groups the further back you trace in the family tree. The instinct of the individual to know himself as an ego surrounded by the concentric circles of identifiable groups (household, family, clan, branch, tribe) means that the force of the segmentary mindset even reaches individual families, for instance when a father has several wives and the sons see themselves in groups according to their mothers. The fiercest loyalty (though few would accept the idea of such gradations) is for 'uterine siblings', then for other siblings, then the families of uncles and so on until the wider group descending from the common ancestor five generations back, and then to larger sections of tribe, tribe and confederation as appropriate. Finally, tribal Arabs of bedouin stock feel a bond of common heritage which distinguishes them from those who are outsiders, the farmers, villagers and townsmen. Within their whole world view, gradated ideas of separateness, polarity, counterpoint and antiphony sit at the roots of social outlook and practice.

The mercy of this system (and system is the observer's word for it: there is no Arabic terminology) is that it assures for both the groups and the individuals, looking across at their opposing segment, a strong equality. Each is responsible for his own and together they stand on equal footing with others. This equality is secure in tribal law, the traditional precedents-based usage of tribal practice which is arbitrated by those accepted as knowledgeable and fair.

William Lancaster, the most sympathetic and acute of contemporary anthropologists of the Middle East, captures both the sense and the practice of these moral ideas ultimately stemming from an identity based on genealogy, in his expression 'the conceptual infrastructure'.[3] The concepts in the conceptual infrastructure are the system of meanings, the shared ethos, the honour code, the genealogy-based identity that frame the moral outlook. The infrastructure is the practical acceptance of these concepts that creates for individuals and groups access to economic, jural, political and social resources. The acceptance allows a 'system' of sponsorship and guarantee that runs informally and allows the individual to

3 See Lancaster, William and Fidelity, 'Tribal Formations in the Arabian Peninsula' *Arabian Archaeology and Epigraphy*, 3, pp. 142–72 (1992).

operate within his group and among other groups who also accept the concepts. The conceptual infrastructure covers tribal Arabia across the peninsula.

Members of tribes today can work their connections and background to land jobs with other governments hundreds of kilometres away from home. The conceptual infrastructure is the medium on which their networks are effective. It all goes back to 'Who am I? My blood tells me who I am.' Principles and practice for dealing with everybody else then flow from this conviction.

More widely, echoes of this system reverberate throughout the Arabic-speaking lands. In history, Islam was spread across the Middle East and beyond by armies coming out of Arabia. The troops in the seventh century were largely of tribal origin. From Morocco to Iraq, tribes and individuals trace their origins back to these upheavals or to the wide travel common within the Islamic community in following centuries. Nostalgia for the drama of Islam's victorious expansion and respect for its Arabian origin lead many to claim some personal attachment to those days, either in their version of family history or in admiration for the hard and lean virtues commonly held to characterize the Arabian tribesman. Hatim al-Tayy'i is still held as a proverbial exemplar of Arab hospitality. His tribe, then centred around Ha'il in today's north-western Saudi Arabia, is now found in northern Syria and Iraq. Hatim lived in the seventh century, a generation before the Prophet Muhammad. Thus the imperative of hospitality, even at great personal inconvenience or cost, the ambition to be generous, the paramount personal dignity of honour or face and, above all, the sanctity of family and respect for the ancestors – these notions and values are still held in esteem across the region. They underpin other more complicated feelings of community in the Arab world. Their traces are found across Mediterranean culture and deep down the east coast of Africa. The Arabs held Spain for seven centuries and ruled Zanzibar until 1861.

Blood is the theme in this inspiration. The practice and the problems are denser. The account of genealogy is impressive. But ask about particular distant individuals in the tree ... 'Who knows?

That was centuries ago! Nobody remembers now.' Genealogies have a way of fitting the need. And in Arabia and the outlying lands, the historical accuracy of these accounts once we are more than a century or so back is an open question. But they are accepted and outsiders' records from a hundred years ago often show the same or very similar versions being told then, as now.

The emotional assertion of the nobility of Arab virtues can, in another mood, in Cairo or Marakesh, Damascus or Mosul, give way to heated vituperation against the tribal mentality, the bedouin thing, the Arabian conservatism and arrogant exclusivity. The greater part of the oil discoveries made in the Middle East in the twentieth century happened in tribal Arabia. Ancestral distrust of the chaotic and unreliable 'Arabs' in smart urban circles is also shot through with jealousy and resentment. The smooth Lebanese and Egyptians, the Syrians and Palestinians who helped the Gulf States develop, find themselves veering from love to hate and back in their relations with the locals. The cultural differences and experiences were wide apart. Blood and segmentation, however, remain at work. Arabs still gang up in rhetoric against perceived intrusions or injustices from outside. The problem of Israel creates a solid platform for this. Jordanians and Syrians have no difficulty in shouting their throats out at national football encounters, but would have a private word of agreement about Palestinians in either team. Palestinians, happy to stay on and invest in Jordan, nurse mutually incompatible feelings about Jordanians. It is a matter of inherited human practice and not institutions, of ego, segment and collective, of individualism and the group, of context and judgement, equality and freedom. The point for them is that it works in a way they understand.

So 'Who is an Arab?' is already a messy question. There are a number of formal answers, but none is final. Membership of the Arab League gives states participation in the Arab project, the aspiration to be today something of what a great past meant. What Somalis and Mauretanians think about this, still needs research, but it is unlikely to fit closely with the from-the-inside-outwards view of someone in Saudi Arabia. Religion supplies an incomplete reply because there are still, though emigration is rapidly depleting them, many Christian communities in the Arab countries and some Jews. There are Druze, Alawites, Yezidis and Shi'ites who do not fit the Sunni Muslim template. Among the Arab populations are many other identities: Kurds, Armenians, Jews, Assyrians and Chaldaeans, Copts, Persians, Turks, Indians, Africans, Turkomans and Circassians or Chechens, to recall only the most obvious. To some extent and in some senses, members of these communities are happy to rub along as Arabs. In other ways, they know exactly how to navigate the grey edges of distinctions, and when it comes to honour, family, marriage and blood, the views become more definite still. A senior Circassian, asked by a friend how Arabs would be reacting to some terrorist outrage, said, 'God knows. Stop one and ask him.'

An established view of modern Middle Eastern history majors on the theme of language as the vector of a new Arab nationalism in the nineteenth century. The Ottomans' practice in government was to allow the many different communities in the empire to look after their own affairs so long as they stood clear of matters of internal security and foreign affairs. Communities were defined by faith and not by language or geography, important though these characteristics might be (especially to our eye). Each *millet* (an Arabic loan word in Turkish meaning faith or confessional community) had latitude to be responsible for its own jurisdiction in religious affairs and thus in many matters of personal status. Arabic was the supreme language in the sphere of sacred studies, but hardly a defining characteristic of particular communities. Most Arabic-speaking subjects of the empire were Sunni Muslims. The term 'Arab' was largely used just for the bedouin of Arabia.[4] The nineteenth-century

---

4 This use is now gone, though it survives among the bedouin themselves. An exchange on chance meeting in the desert: 'Who are you?' 'I am one of these Arabs.' 'Clearly, but of which ones?' And if the reply is, 'These ones', then it is game to the home team and the visitor has lost. Giving away information is how you get caught out in a blood feud. The strangers may have one of your own kind in mind and mean violence.

promotion of Arabic as an intellectual medium outside the context of religion ran in step with a sense of malaise in the empire, an increasing contact with powerful foreigners, interest in their sciences and ideas and a growing sense of independent identity as against the Turkish-speaking people of the empire. The European experience of developing a sense of nationhood was infectious – the emergence of the modern idea of Zionism dates from the mid-nineteenth century. It was a short step for the Arabic-speaking peoples of the empire to conclude that their language gave them identity, that he who spoke Arabic and thought of himself as an Arab was indeed an Arab. Arab nationalism as a political idea gathered steam in the Arabs' encounter with the foreign powers which after the First World War took slices of the defeated empire and became holders of mandates, in effect colonial rulers.

This is an unmistakable narrative and illuminates so much that has happened in the so-called modern era. An important theme in the story is the aspirational aspect of the identity. The convictions about blood (whether strictly accurate or not) run with a sense that beliefs and values, as a horizon of ambition, define where I am now and thus who I am. The macro picture, however, can be seductive, the talk of modernism and nationalism heady. In returning to the dimension of the individual, we find the insistent influence of older habits and outlooks. The rulers who are inheritors of those Arab nationalist and, later, revolutionary platforms, now show little reticence in grooming their sons to succeed them in power. By watching what people do, rather than what they say, we discover that continuities have survived from before the turbulence of the twentieth century. Identity, it seems, is not so easy to shift away from its chosen anchorages, blood and family. It is, however, subject to a major pull, one the Ottomans understood. And that pull is creed. Religion supplies its own statement of values and conviction that also propose an identity. This is the subject of the next chapter, but the to-ing and fro-ing, the tidal relationship, between the ocean of faith and the mainland of genealogy, is thematic to the Arabs' story. Today, the flux seems to be going in the direction of faith, as the Arab vogue comes to the end of its current phase.

The difficult case in defining the Arab is always Egypt. Egypt is the most populous Arab country and the vitality of its culture and personality has made it a dominant element in the Middle East. Its Islamic university, al-Azhar, still has enormous prestige in the teaching of Islamic sciences and religion and Arabic is fundamental to all of these. Nasser's radio station, 'Voice of the Arabs', had impact, one way or the other, in every home throughout the 1950s and 1960s. Egyptian writers set the standard for literary achievement and expatriate Egyptian schoolmasters dominated education and syllabuses throughout the Middle East. Egyptian writers have had a pre-eminent influence in the turmoil of radical Islam since the mid-nineteenth century. And yet, Egypt's Arab-ness is qualified. Egyptians take pride in their pre-Arab civilization (the Arabs conquered Egypt during the Muslim armies' expansion from the Hijaz in 639–642) and they are sensitive that they are also a major African state. When it suits the Egyptian government to play the African card in international politics, no one is surprised. The Egyptian default position is undoubtedly deep inside a consciousness of being Arab. Yet it is subject to mood-swings, as was clear during President Sadat's period of estrangement from the Arab world after his visit to Jerusalem in 1977. The sure assessment is that Egyptians are Egyptian. Categories which may enclose that humble truth can be hazardous. Further east, the generalizations will be steadier. In the west, in Libya, Tunisia, Algeria and Morocco other influences also play their part. The Berbers and Saharan tribes have their say, but these lands were not originally as heavily populated with settled people as was the Nile valley, and the overlay of Arab conquest and migrants took firmer hold.

In the central Arab lands, from Syria and Iraq to the Yemen and Oman, there are other distinctions to be made. The saline flat coastal country which lies at the west of the United Arab Emirates, cutting it off from Qatar, is inhospitable and empty. It is called the *Bainunah*, 'the dividing marches'. Called this since long before the inauguration of today's states, the *Bainunah* in reality marks a division between two genealogical systems and, to a considerable extent, two cultures within the inner Arab family. The dividing line can be traced westwards across the peninsula to the Hijaz mountains and Jedda on the coast.

North of this line are the sons of Isma'il (Ishmael), the son of Hagar the servant of Sarah, the wife of Abraham. According to the story in Genesis,[5] Hagar who at Sarah's instigation bore Abraham the son, had a major falling out with Sarah and took off into the desert. There God hears her lament for her child. She is met by an angel who saves them both. The boy is named Isma'il (deriving in the Hebrew version from *Yishma' el* – 'God Hears') and, the narrative continues, 'God was with the boy. He grew up and made his home in the desert, and became an archer'.[6] The Koranic narrative carries less detail, but Ibrahim and his son Isma'il are linked together in covenant with God to purify his house, the sanctuary of the *Ka'abah* at Mecca, as a place of prayer. Isma'il, as the eldest son, is always mentioned in the Koran before Isaac and Jacob. The Prophet is told by the angel to mention Isma'il in the book as he was true to his promise and a prophet, telling his people to pray and give alms. He was pleasing to his Lord.[7] This venerable and patriarchal figure had, according to Genesis, 12 sons who were the heads of 12 tribes, paralleling the structure of the people of Israel. The generations from Isma'il – 'Adnan, Ma'd, Nizar and his two sons Mudar and Rabi'ah – give us the names from which the northern tribes claim descent.

In the south, descent comes from a more ancient figure, Qahtan, identified with Yoktan in Genesis,[8] the descendant through five generations of Noah. Tradition ascribes to Qahtan patriarchal status for all the peoples of the south, though modern scholars are more cautious about the complex demographics of the Yemen and the presence of Hamitic and other distinct races.

The southerners are known as *al-'Arab al-'Aribah* (the pure Arabs) and the northerners as *al-'Arab al-Must'aribun* (incomers). Whatever the historicity of all this, the fact that the Prophet

5 See Genesis 16 and 21.
6 See Genesis 21.20.
7 See *Surat Miriam*: 54–55.
8 See Genesis 25–26.

Muhammad came from the stock of 'Adnan and Isma'il and the Muslim community spread north to kingdom in Damascus and thence to empire in Baghdad, gave a boost to the fortunes of the northerners.

Overall, the idea survived that the real Arabs, whatever their genealogical roots, were the bedouin and, certainly to outsiders, the bedouin remained a type apart, whether they were from north or south. On the inside, prejudices were maintained. I remember Wilfred Thesiger having lunch with a senior shaikh from the enormous Shammar tribe of northern Arabia. Wilfred had been praising his bedouin friends in the Empty Quarter, the heroes of his book, *Arabian Sands*. The shaikh asked me in Arabic (which Wilfred had by this time forgotten), 'Why does he go on about those wild things in the south? Their tribes are only a few hundred strong; they live in a closed world and have closed minds. They are unknown and unknowing. We on the other hand . . . ' Segmentation was kicking in hard. Wilfred's Rashid tribesmen were, like the shaikh himself, Qahtanis: the Shammar stem from the Tayy in Iraq and Syria, Qahtani stock which moved up north many centuries ago. Blood creates many tricky home truths and they are not necessarily keen on our knowing about them.

The Arab's attitude to horses is an illustration of the esteem for blood and his trust in it. Arabs love horses and respect them. The Arab mare, bred in the desert and treated on equal terms with the members of the household, enjoys the same dignity and elitism in pedigree as the humans around her. Tradition inevitably supplies a story that the five principal families of Arab horse trace their origins back to six horses released by King David after he noticed that his love of horses was keeping him from his attention to his prayers.[9] As among humans, these traditions simply express and bolster a remarkable commitment to careful breeding to preserve purity and reliability. The bedouin relied on their horses in their raids and bred strains which would perform well in these ordeals. The result was a horse credited with being the foundation of English thoroughbred

9 A note of this appears in the Koran – see *Surat Sad*: 30–33.

blood-lines and the toast of racetracks across the Indian empire. Those Englishmen who bought horses from Arabia recognized that accounts of pedigree by those who had actually bred the horse were never disputed. The integrity of the horse's blood-line was but an extension of the integrity of the Arab's own breeding. Tweedie, British Consul-General in Baghdad in the mid-nineteenth century, a great horse enthusiast and the author of a monograph on Arab horses, noted a bedouin's sarcastic comment that the people of the towns did not know their own genealogies like the bedouin did, but with the way the townsmen covered up their women's faces, who could ever be sure who his mother was!

The attachment to blood in the unforgiving and relentless environment of Arabia was no pretension, but rather a response to the demand that both individuals and the group be fit for purpose – survival and upholding honour which derived from integrity of identity. One of Thesiger's favourite aphorisms derived from his huge experience of living with tribal people, 'The harder the life, the finer the type.' By this, Wilfred would have by no means meant that a hard life should be prescribed, but rather that the observation was the inescapable conclusion of what he had seen – and subliminally that careful breeding also delivered the type. This deep discipline of the desert is respected and even imitated by those who have not lived on the desert's anvil. It is both instinct and sentiment and it colours the outlook of Arab societies far from Arabia.

The Arabic adjective '*asil* is used for someone of pure blood. It is also used for horses and camels of sound pedigree. The word covers ideas from 'original' and 'genuine' to 'authentic', 'pure' and 'noble'. The moral element in these ideas is striking and, in the Arab world, non-negotiable

Chapter 3

Religion

In a collection of writings he called *al-Takmilah* (The Summing-Up), King 'Abd Allah I, the founder of the Hashimite kingdom of Jordan, set himself a number of questions in a piece headed 'An Arab speaks about the Arabs'. He begins like this,

> 'Who are you?'
> 'I am an Arab. I am descended from the Arabs and I take pride in them.'
> 'What makes you proud?'
> 'My religion and my descent.'
> 'What is your religion?'
> 'My religion is Islam. My Lord is Allah and my prophet is Muhammad, May God bless him and grant him salvation.'

The king comes straight out with what really matters to him and what he knows will matter most to his readers. His statement contains subtleties and these will not be lost on his readers. The subtleties reveal a paradox. His point about blood alternates with what he says about his religion. They are closely intertwined. He has no need, of course, to remind his readers that his own descent from the Hashimite house includes, within the family, Muhammad, the Prophet himself.[1] At the same time, the king links himself with the Arabs as the people of the Muslim community. The Islamic apprehension of God is of the Absolute. The universal call of the

---

1 'Abd Allah's father, Husain, before he declared himself King of the Hijaz (and got removed by Ibn Sa'ud), was the Sharif, and ruler, of Mecca. 'Abd Allah, in the aftermath of the Arab Revolt against the Ottomans, persuaded Churchill at the Cairo conference in 1921 to create for him the Emirate of Transjordan and a kingdom in Iraq for his brother Faisal. The eponymous founder of the Hashimite line was Hashim bin 'Abd Manaf, the Prophet's great-grandfather.

Prophet to submit to God's absolute will transcends the natural human boundaries of clan and nationality.

The paradox in assenting to these two attitudes at once, the particularity of blood and the universality of a religious belief, has been present since the earliest years of Islam. Should the successor to Muhammad be a member of the Prophet's family, or alternatively the man best able to discharge the duties of leadership after the Prophet had died? This controversy marked the early caliphate[2] in Medina and the controversy has arisen and gone quiet again over the centuries. But the enigma has never been resolved, or disappeared: the attention to blood pulls one way; the strongly egalitarian instincts of Arabian tribal society pull another. The latter, the direction in fact chosen by the Muslim community in electing Abu Bakr as the Prophet's successor, is the direction which rides more easily with commitment to the equality of all believers in the face of the utter otherness of God the Creator.

The otherness of God is absolute, yet to the Muslim Arab, the reality of God in the world, the truths God revealed to man in the revelation of the Koran, and man's accountability to God for his response to these truths, are all as plain and as beneficial as the air he breathes to stay alive. So, in the Arab world, God remains socialized in a way we have not seen in Europe since perhaps before the Enlightenment. God is omnipresent in the community and not, as for those in the West, simply reckoned to be as a matter of personal belief. The implications are vast.

The Semitic people of the Middle East have, humanly speaking, given the world three great religions, developed from what they have experienced as decisive interventions in human affairs by God, the one God, the God of Abraham, who chose from among their number prophets and messengers to announce his will for his creation. Whatever atheists and agnostics make of these assertions,

2 *Khalifah* in Arabic means successor or 'viceregent' and, since the Prophet's death, 'successor of the Prophet of God.' The caliph was the head of the Muslim community. The title was assumed by various leaders including the Ottoman sultans. The title fell into disuse when the Ottoman empire was abolished after the First World War. Restoring it remains the aim of some of the Islamist fringe groups.

we are left with an inescapable impression of a Semitic genius for religious thought. The professor at an English university quoted in the introduction to R. K. Harrison's Hebrew course, who always began his initial lecture on the Hebrew language with the words, 'Gentlemen, this is the language which God spoke', would have met with a trenchant comment had a Muslim student been present: the Koran in several places makes much of being an Arabic revelation, a right guidance to mankind in Arabic. And it is a fundamental belief for many Muslims that the Koran was uncreated, a divine communication from beyond time, given complete to the archangel Gabriel and passed verbatim to Muhammad. In that sense the Koran is sometimes referred to by outsiders as the 'miracle of Islam'. Arabic thus also has the distinction of being the language 'which God spoke'. Consequently, many Muslims reject the idea of translation of the Koran. A close translation can only be seen as 'explanatory'.

A remarkable aspect of the Semitic response to these revelations was the effort to reorder thinking about God from the particular to the universal, to move from our God to the God of the whole wide world. For each religion, coping with the universality of the other two versions remains unfinished business. Here the primitive origins of Semitic religion are instructive.

The people of Israel are set by God to be a channel for his grace (see text at note 1 of Chapter 2), but the descendants of Abraham through Isaac and Jacob, the 12 tribes stemming from Jacob's sons, struggle with their competing ambitions. The echoes of the problems of segmentation are unmistakable. Questions of inclusion are heatedly debated. After the return of the Jews from captivity in Babylon, the returnees are at odds with those who stayed behind. Mary Douglas, in her *In the Wilderness* and *Jacob's Tears,*[3] shows how the priestly editors of Numbers and Leviticus hold out against those seeking a more exclusive identity, for an understanding of religion as a mission to all, irrespective of descent. The matter is

---

3 Douglas, Mary, *In the Wilderness: The Doctrine of Defilement in the Book of Numbers* (Oxford, Oxford Unversity Press, 2001), and *Jacob's Tears: The Priestly Work of Reconciliation* (Oxford, Oxford Unversity Press, 2004).

intense and, to some critics, unresolved, but the mission to be a sign to all peoples is never wholly put aside.

In the New Testament, in St Matthew's account of the Incarnation, the generations from Abraham to Joseph, the husband of Mary, are counted at 42. The arrival of the three wise men to pay homage to the holy child has traditionally been taken as a sign of his mission to the whole world. In St Luke's gospel, when Joseph and Mary take Jesus to be presented at the temple, Simeon takes the child in his arms and speaks of him as 'a light to lighten the gentiles ... '[4] The mission to the world is taken up by Peter and Paul and the other disciples. The young Church spreads to Asia Minor and to Rome.

In Arabic *Islam* means submission. The call in the Koran to submit to God is first made to the Arabs but explicitly also to the world at large. There can only be believers and without distinction among them. The Koran calls for respect and tolerance to be shown to the 'People of the Book', the Jews and Christians, for they worship the same God of Ibrahim, Isma'il, Musa (Moses) and the other prophets. The castigation of the errors into which the Jews and Christians are said to have fallen in their beliefs and practices, is fierce in places, but the underlying relationship with the earlier revelations is clear and held in respect until now. The assertion is simply that Muhammad is the 'seal of the prophets': that the revelation of which he was the human mouthpiece, is complete and final.

Originally, in the earliest religion of the Semites, matters stood quite differently. In his Burnett Lectures given in 1887–89,[5] W. Robertson Smith examines this pre-prophetic religious tradition. The interest of his researches for us today, quite apart from the enduring authority of his teaching and insights, is that he also describes the background to the cultural milieu in which Muhammad pursued his mission to the pagan Arabs of the peninsula. Robertson Smith found that religion for the early Semites was cult and practice, rather than doctrine and belief. Each clan and tribe

4 St Luke 2.32.
5 Robertson Smith, William, *The Religion of the Semites* (London, 1889).

recognized gods which they understood to be part of their extended community: family gods, family persons and family animals. For the flocks and herds were integral to their microcosm, their particular version, their understanding, of creation. And the deities had their own place in this natural and supernatural order. Thus religion was identity; and ritual was affirmation of this identity. The gods were on 'our side' in conflict; and when peace broke out, a coalescence of gods might arise from new tribal and family alliances. Gods also had geographical affinities, as did the lower order of spiritual being, jinns or genies. The emergence of principal deities in ancient Arabia and the association of lesser deities with particular places had their origins in such customs and outlooks.[6]

A stately old Coptic lady once chided me for an attitude which she said was typical of the English visitor to Egypt. 'Oh you English,' she said, 'you are always fascinated by the Muslims and so sympathetic to them. And why not? But you all fail to see that the outlook of the people of your own religion is universal. Muslims are particular.' This comment, of course, would be outrageous to a Muslim and would been seen as an affront to doctrine, but in so far as individual Muslims can fall short of their religion's ideals, the impression is recognizable, if a little harsh. It is true that Muslims have very little appetite for inter-faith dialogue. Ambassadors from Islamic states do not often turn up to state occasions held in churches. But it is also true that individuals who are not uncommon, are quite ready to do these things. The arrival of a Saudi Arabian representative at the funeral of Pope John Paul II in 2005 was unprecedented. Christians are familiar to them from the Christian communities in the Middle East. Arab Christian women who marry Muslims are able to continue with the practice of their religion and are respected for it. A nun who visited us from home when we were in Jordan came with us on a visit to the desert and got caught up in long conversation with the wife of a bedouin shaikh who wanted to know all about her beliefs and her commitment to her vocation. But it is true that the

6 See Hoyland, Robert, *The Arabs and Arabia – From the Bronze Age to the Coming of Islam* (London, Routledge, 2001), pp. 157 *et seq.*

temper of the times and the prominence in the Western media of Muslim extremists both obscure the widespread tolerance of ordinary Muslim Arabs. If there is an impression of narrowness, or lack of interest in what lies outside the Muslim community, its roots may lie amid the old instincts of religious identity cohabiting with genealogical identity and the deep detachment about what goes on outside the extended circle of kinship.

From earliest times, non-Muslims living in the Muslim community were clearly outsiders. They had a client (Arabic: *dhimmi*) status with codified obligations (e.g. to pay more taxes) and limited rights. A number of practical disabilities in today's Arab states are still the lot of non-Muslim subjects[7] They are unlikely to rise to high rank in military or public service. The higher levels of the judiciary will be closed since, in most countries, the law derives in varying degrees from the *Shari'ah*, the legal code drawn from the Koran. A paradoxical illustration of this is the ancient practice of absolute rulers employing non-Arabs, those well outside the circle of a possible marriage alliance, even non-Muslims, in the highest ranks of civil and court service, close to the centre of power. The dynasty of Barmakid viziers at the start of the 'Abbasid caliphate in Baghdad were Persians; Armenians and Greeks were notable in the ranks of the closest advisers to the Ottoman sultans; the praetorian guard of Janissaries at Istanbul were traditionally made up from military schools which recruited or captured young Christian boys from a young age and converted them. In modern times, Circassians have long enjoyed honourable positions at the Hashimite court in Jordan. The point is that these people, even when Muslims, had no powerful family or social bloc behind them. They could not, of themselves, pose a threat to power in a society where identity, we can almost say legitimacy, derives from blood *and* religion and vice versa.

In the early years of Islam this instinct for the precedence of family had major repercussions for the future of the community. When the Prophet died in 632, Abu Bakr, the first caliph or

---

7 The Lebanon is an exception due to its greater balance of confessional communities.

successor, was elected. His assumed and de facto acclaimed successor, 'Umar, was assassinated. The community elected 'Uthman who was also assassinated. The fourth caliph, 'Ali, the prophet's cousin and son-in-law, was also elected. But the elections were controversial because there was a strong opinion that the caliphate should have already passed directly down the line of the Prophet's own family. This party had wanted 'Ali from the start. When he was elected against the opposition of, among others, the Prophet's widow 'Aishah, 'Ali had to contend with the internal tensions of the community – those arising from the murder of his predecessor, 'Uthman, and those deriving from the hostility of outlying governors appointed by 'Umar, the second caliph. Not the least of these was Mu'awiyah, the governor of Damascus who would later take over from him as caliph. 'Ali went off to Kufa, today's Najaf in Iraq, and had to fight Mu'awiyah. An arbitration forced on 'Ali by Mu'awiyah by subterfuge went against 'Ali. A group of 'Ali's troops, outraged that the caliph should accept arbitration and this outcome, departed and one of their number later assassinated him in 661. 'Ali's followers who believed that the caliphate should remain in the family of the Prophet, maintained their opposition to Mu'awiyah who now proclaimed himself caliph in Damascus. They stayed in Iraq and developed their own schismatic group. This, the Shi'at 'Ali (The Party of 'Ali), is the Shi'ah we know today.

Today, we tend to associate the Shi'ah with Iran because there are 70 million Iranians and Khomeini's revolution was a big political event in the twentieth century.[8] But this early schism in the Islamic community was Arab and not Iranian. It was a dispute about the role of the Prophet's descendants in the government of the community,

---

8 Khomeini articulated a new doctrine, *Velayat-i Faqih* ('the vicegerency of the jurisprudent/theologian'). He taught that the Shi'i clergy were the vicegerents of God on earth. It followed that the supreme religious authority in the Shi'i hierarchy (the Sunnis have no similar structures) should be the supreme leader of the state. Though Shi'i in thought and teaching, this revolution gave encouragement to a wider rising tide of Islamist activists which had been noticeable during the 1970s – see Chapter 8.

the relationship between blood, power and the universal agenda of the faith. The Iranian connection developed much later.

The Shi'i community in Iraq pushed the perimeter of the Arab world northwards and eastwards and increasingly mixed with non-Arab peoples. They encountered and were exposed to more and more of the influences of foreign religions. Whether or not derived from ideas in Zoroastrianism and Mazdaism, the Shi'ah developed the belief that the *imams*, descendants of the line of 'Ali, had special access to divine grace. Thus their knowledge was exceptional and therefore so was their authority.

Those whose allegiance stayed with the new caliph in Damascus became known as Sunnis. They followed, in their own estimation, the custom, the *Sunnah*, of the Prophet. While there are still majority populations of the Shi'ah in Iraq, in Bahrain and Yemen, and significant groups in the Levant and Morocco and along the shore of the Gulf, the rest of the Arabs are predominantly Sunnis.

Blood, religion and power – these are our terms and categories of thought. Our own religions have long histories of involvement in what we call secular power, but they have also stood in opposition to power. Islam as a creed has had an enormous influence on culture and it created a multinational civilization. Most importantly, it has remained a way of life for the laity, and not a church. With the exception of the Shi'iah, a hierarchical clergy did not grow up. Islam was the inspiration for statecraft and the leader of the state often asserted himself as religious leader. It is true that the leader could not alter the terms of the *Shari'ah* and this was interpreted by *qadis*, judges learned in the religious texts, but he nonetheless appointed the judges. Consequently, a good many Muslims, while recognizing the language – the distinctions to be made between personal, religious and political matters – do not accept that these distinctions are applicable to the Islamic community. A good many reject the notion of religion and state as opposing, or polarized, elements in society. The difficulty for us of these categories of thought can be seen in the use of the word *shaikh* to mean a religious elder, as well as tribal leader. On this view which is rooted in Koranic prescriptions, Islam is a comprehensive programme for life. It envelopes both the project of how to live in community, making provisions for matters of personal status, marriage, inheritance and so on, and also for penalties for crime. Islam also addresses the aspirations of the individual in the interior life, the realm of prayer and a personal relationship with God.

A great desire for yet closer personal encounter with God in this life was the inspiration for Islamic mystics, the Sufis. The core message of the Sufi is emphatically about the love which God has for his creation and each individual creature. The soul, purified of its self-seeking inclinations and burnished by fidelity to God's will, can become a reflection of God's bright love and thus a channel for it in his world. The soul, a window of glass, stained and opaque with sin, can be cleaned and ascetically polished so that God comes through all the clearer. And this is no pious, but ultimately selfish, cultivation of the self, but a journey towards release – to allow God to release the soul in an ecstasis of nature to exist for others and for his will which is an outpouring of generous love.

The Sufi tradition shares much common ground with mystical traditions in other religions. Judaic and Christian traditions and, to some extent, those further east speak of similar themes. Clearly the Sufi is not concerned with power in this world and this perhaps may have coloured the motives of the Ottoman sultans who gave official support to the Sufi orders. It is hard not to speculate whether those hard-headed and shrewd men of power saw that the Sufis' influence coincided with a useful purpose: softening the appeal of those voices which called for more rigorous social, even political, action in conforming to the traditions of the Prophet. Such voices represented a reproach to the Ottomans' practice.

Such voices, admittedly way off in the Syrian provinces and beyond in the deserts of Arabia, had reach and were articulate. Ahmad Ibn Taimiyah (1268–1328), a scholar of the Hanbali school,[9] had sharpened the pen of puritanical zeal with his preaching, writings and fatwahs, criticizing many substantial figures in the Islamic

---

9 There are four canonical schools of law: the *Shafi'i*, *Maliki*, *Hanafi* and *Hanbali*, named after their founding imams and jurists.

tradition, fulminating against philosophers (especially those who got involved with Greek philosophy), Sufi veneration of dead 'saints', the tolerance of Jewish and Christian religion and the maintenance of synagogues and churches. Ibn Taimiyah's voice resonates through the tradition of Islamic activists and radicals, notably, in Arabia, Muhammad ibn 'Abd al-Wahhab (1703–87) and, in Egypt, Muhammad 'Abduh (1849–1905), and has remained a source of powerful encouragement and inspiration among the Islamists of our own day.

From the end of the Ottoman empire, the Sufi tradition went into a long decline. The main roads of Islamic discussion and dispute became dominated by the harder-edged and, in our terms more political, neo-Hanbalis, the Muslim Brothers and others groups like them. Hasan al-Banna, the founder of the Muslim Brothers, had started off as a Sufi and his organizational genius made a successful evolutionary bridge between the popular quietist attachment to the Sufi order, *tariqah*, and the *jama'ah*, or Islamic Group, the zealous and sectarian oppositionists with which we are so familiar today. Sufis gathered round a shaikh, a local master himself part of a wider distributed network of the order; and similarly the Islamic groups are localized associations around an *amir* who may be part of some wider loose network. The social structures, reminiscent of the family group and wider tribe, are an adaptation of the 'conceptual infrastructure' (see p. 16) of the tribal Arabs.

Ibn Taimiyah wrote at the time of the Mongol incursions into the Near East. Muhammad ibn 'Abd al-Wahhab would have been well aware of the arrival of the British in India. Muhammad 'Abduh was profoundly affected by the traumatic arrival of European 'modernity' in Egypt in the shape of Napoleon in 1798. Anthropologists show us that culture is developed, strengthened and, to some extent, defined in adversity. The strong personality of the Arabic-speaking Muslim community was bound to react deeply to foreign military success. It did and it sought renewal and reinvigoration by returning to its sources – literalism in its response to revelation and the traditions, the recorded personal sayings (*hadith*) and practice (*sunnah*) of the Prophet. Implicit in this return to source was some rejection of intervening religious authority and teaching which in any way strayed from immediate dependence on these first sources, and, of course, a spirited criticism of contemporary rulers who cooperated or colluded with the new external and non-Muslim powers. Among these rulers, the revolutionary regimes, dressed in Western khaki and promoting the kind of nationalism which echoed the strongly secular systems of Europe and the Soviet Union, were particular targets of the radicals' hostility. In Egypt in 1954, the Muslim Brothers tried to kill Nasser. In 1981 successor but different Muslim radicals killed Sadat.

Albert Hourani's *A History of the Arab Peoples* ends with a chapter entitled 'A Disturbance of Spirits' – a brilliant phrase capturing the temper of the times since 1967, itself a date full of humiliation and defeat for the Arabs. But Hourani concentrated on the social and political drivers at work. Touching on the Islamic dimension of the post-1967 mood, Hourani focuses, perhaps fairly, on the differences distinguishing the activities of 'fundamentalist' groups in different countries. But he summarizes, 'Leadership of Islamic movements therefore tended to be in the hands of laymen, converted members of the modern educated elite. Such movements did not have the sanctity conferred by leaders of inherited and recognized piety and learning; they were political parties competing with others.'[10] Hourani's book was published in 1991. More than a decade later, the slight misgivings which many felt at the time about his analysis of the religious movements, seem justified. Surely more than this has been going on?

Here we are inhibited by our contemporary diffidence. The matter of Islam is fraught. Hourani was right – there is a disturbance of spirits and it is visible in the promotion of local dissent to the strategic level of international security: the hard problem of terrorism and the so-called 'war' led by the United States to counter it. But the high probability is that Muslims will be dissatisfied with our attempts to understand the present situation of Islam. That, however, does not absolve us from a need to try to understand. Even if

---

10 *A History of the Arab Peoples,* p. 458.

the experience and aspirations of Muslim communities are felt to be misjudged by our efforts, we have to try to understand.

The non-Muslim who looks closely at Islam and listens to the wide range of Muslim voices who will each assert a more 'correct version', is left with two areas of profound uncertainty.

Firstly there is knowledge and its fruit which is authority. We approach the topic of knowledge from different angles and we mean different things. For the Muslim, the divinely given fact of revelation and its attested text presents an immediate challenge: 'Do I know the text, or not? It exists and is there, whether I do, or not. What is my relationship with it?' Thus, as a few generations ago, young Roman Catholic boys whose parents wanted them to have a chance of ordination to the priesthood, would send them in their early teens to seminaries, so Muslim parents might send their children to Koranic schools at an earlier age where they would be taught the Koran by heart and then graduate to studies of the tradition. Knowledge of the text in this way gives authority because religious teaching derives from the text.

Though often hearing criticism of learning by rote, this method never caused me special difficulty. At school we were made to learn by heart long passages of Demosthenes to inculcate a feeling for the idiom of ancient Greek. When I was living in Cairo and wanted to renew my study of the Koran, I sought out a shaikh (in the religious sense) who would agree to give me lessons in recitation, studying the major interpretations of the text, in grammar and also in calligraphy.[11] This dignified old man with enormous glasses (Koran school is often the lot of children who are blind or hard of seeing) entered into the spirit of my needs and we sat together for two sessions a week for nearly three years. Slowly, it dawned on me that this man who knew not a word of a foreign language, had had a formation which in his case had resulted in a tolerant and benign outlook on the world which I could only describe as liberal. I could

11 The Arabs do not like representation of the forms created by God, and their graphic art centres on design and calligraphy. Calligraphy, with their respect for the word spoken to them by God, is their equivalent in some sense to iconography.

by no means say that he was not highly educated. He deeply impressed me. Sometimes, at the end of our session, I would open the Koran at random and read a few words. He would then from memory complete the verse and offer to continue. He just knew the 6,236 verses of the Koran by heart and no mistake about it. The Arabic term for someone who has graduated to a high level of expertise in religious matters, far higher than my shaikh, is *'alim*, the present participle of the verb meaning 'to know'.

The would-be Islamic scholar faces a formidable body of knowledge which he must master. The commitment demanded is great and the formation contains its own fierce asceticism. The first printing press in the Arab world was opened in Cairo in 1828. The elitism of this tradition of knowledge was thus enormous and the prestige of the *'ulama*[12] in the great universities of the Islamic world was correspondingly great. They could not only read and write, but they *knew*.

One of the great discourses of the Islamic tradition is about 'imitation' or *taqlid*. A sympathetic view of this long-standing question would hold up and support the requirement to know and have respect for the great authorities of the past who transmitted the accepted interpretations of the text of the Koran and the written traditions (*hadith*) of the Prophet. The unsympathetic and opposing view criticizes such a blind adherence to other and (merely) human judgements, asserting the need for each to form his own view, well within the boundaries of orthodoxy, inspired by deep faith and put to the test of virtue in outcome. This debate, fluctuating across the centuries, has had a tendency to return to the powerful gravitational field of those authorities who assembled the canon of the Prophetic traditions (*hadith*), and ultimately, of course, to the unshakeable text of revelation, the Koran itself. Thus literalism in response to revelation has remained a characteristic theme which we, particularly and naturally, notice because our own tradition is so different.

---

12 *'Ulama* is used for the plural of *'alim* and stands for the 'periti', those well versed in the religious sciences.

The literalism derives from a desire to know, and stick as closely as possible to, the objective truths of revelation.

Generally speaking, the *'ulama* have not been put to the test of dialogue and argument with philosophers and scientists in a way we might assume. There was, of course, an era when this occurred. We are indebted to the mediaeval Islamic scholars of Baghdad and Spain for the transmission to us of many important classical texts. Thomas Aquinas in thirteenth-century Paris was much concerned with Islamic schools of thought, considering and arguing with their propositions and insights. But that era ended and has left limited traces. With the disappearance of the *mu'tazili* school of rationalist thinkers, many philosophical questions were left aside. Do we, for instance, obtain our knowledge of values simply and subjectively from revelation, or do we derive it rationally from defining by reason the values naturally inherent in humans? The argument went to the more subjective of these two views and that was that. Critical analysis of what we know, has thus tended to concentrate on the quality of tradition, the soundness of the source chains (a problem, in fact, closed some centuries ago), rather than on the content of the material.

In the modern Arab world, sciences and philosophy have grown as disciplines quite separate from the fields of religious study. The avowed specialization of the *'ulama* and the demands of the knowledge they were seeking, at the least left them little time or scope for such interdisciplinary engagement. The modernizing aspirations of those committed to the sciences, medicine, engineering or economics had a tone of secularism, implicit in the texts and papers available on these topics from their contemporary origin in the West or socialist East. For the early nationalist and revolutionary regimes, the study of science was a mission in the service of developing backward societies and making them more independent. This was not a primarily religious purpose. Their style was secularist (how else to compete with the West?) and they kept their *'ulama* on a tight rein, supporting the interests of the regimes. They neglected the need to renew and acclimatize the techniques of religious education.

The resulting cultural divisions which grew up in the Arab world in the twentieth century, faced, in the century's later years, a certain confusion as the harbingers of globalization took hold. The assertion of the authority of learning and knowledge became a weaker voice as the people, and particularly the young, were faced with rapidly expanding possibilities for different fields of knowledge and a different learning. As people sought help with modern dilemmas, the questions to which the *'ulama* were exposed were trickier. And the answers they gave, suggested the limitations of the religious men's experience.

Importantly, in the burgeoning bureaucracies of the new Arab nations, the *'ulama* could not escape some compromise and collusion with the demands of power and, generally, far from liberal regimes. This involvement was hardly voluntary. The *'ulama* staffed the religious courts, the state-owned mosques and the religious faculties of state-funded universities. Even al-Azhar in Cairo, the great mosque and university opened in 972, had to lie close to the regime. Its *Shaikh*, or dean, was effectively the senior Islamic figure in the land and enjoyed enormous prestige and moral authority throughout the *'ulama* of the Islamic world. But knowledge by itself had become no longer an adequate defence. Relevance now mattered as well, if authority were to appear justified to the ideologically restive faithful. The recourse to now widely available primary sources and to revelation thus became a two-edged sword, cutting both at the great corpus of Islamic knowledge and the docile traditions by which most lived. Now, others could read the books and take what they wanted from them.

Three trends became explicit. As Hourani shrewdly pointed out at the time, the powerful rhetoric was the voice of the activist radicals, in most cases autodidacts and of limited real attainment against the traditional criteria of knowledge. Secondly, empowered by travel and media, both activists and some genuinely learned dissidents were able to continue their missions and preaching from the safer distance of refuge in more congenial, conservative states like those of the Gulf and Saudi Arabia. Linked to this and thirdly, there was the experience of those who got away to Europe and America. As had been Ibn Taimiyah, some significant personalities (e.g. Sayid Qutb in the United States and Muhammad 'Abduh in France) had been animated and impelled by their experience of the outside world to a more strident critique of contemporary Muslim society and a deeper recourse to the authority of the virtuous early community in the century following the death of the Prophet. To their number was soon added large populations of immigrants, refugees and political asylum seekers who, in the alien milieu of Europe and the United States, took their radical conservativism out to yet new boundaries. This, of course, caused new dimensions of tension between Arab regimes who wanted these radicals returned, and those Western states who gave the radicals a roof of tolerance and freedom to print and broadcast. Their sense of isolation was often increased as the new and avant-garde positions they adopted separated them from the more traditional and easy going attitudes of their own families at home in the region.

The underlying riddle for us as outsiders is how to place these now sharply differing voices in some pattern around the central idea of Islam. The traditional and venerable criterion of knowledge as some metric for gauging the authority of these voices is obscured by the volume and diversity of the debate. A tolerant and, in some ways, easy-going approach to Islam for the majority of people is becoming itself controversial. And so the appeals to the basic text of revelation get louder. Rejection of *taqlid*, a self-asserting right to speak abroad, and a suspicion of the frailty of conventional clerical obedience to governments, have lifted the volume well above the level of comfort. In the contest of knowledge, the ropes have come off the ring. The point is made by the common rejoinder when this issue is discussed, that 'Islam is what I mean by it ... my Islam'.

The second striking theme of uncertainty for outsiders is closely linked to this crisis of knowledge and authority. The high culture of 'Abbasid or Andalusian Islam seems at this distance to have had a strong spirit of tolerance. The historicity of this, in terms of the actual experience of non-Muslims living inside the Muslim community, would now be a difficult subject for research. The fact remains that apart from the experience of the days of colonial influence, pluralism in a sense which we should understand, has not been developed as a religiously or politically respectable position. The lines of precedence and privilege were always set in favour of the dominant Muslim regime and its Muslim subjects. Christian or Jewish subjects might, or might not, have enjoyed considerable freedom from daily unpleasantness, but their equality was never assumed or allowed as a principle. We have already touched on the notable exceptions of favoured servants of the ruler and court. They were indeed exceptions. St Augustine's dictum that 'there are many wolves within the fold and many sheep without' gives us the spirit of an outlook which lies behind our own arguments for the acceptance of dissent and contradiction. This intellectual framework is not present in the Islamic world.

The individual Arab, remote from the scholastic disputes of the *'ulama,* has probably always simply found his own space. His fidelity to Islamic teaching and values has continued within the possibilities of his own nature and inclination. He is aware that he is part of a grand and, for him, ultimately true, divine programme for humanity. His religious utterances are generally gentle and friendly. Faced, however, with printed argument based on texts, with broadcast debate about the extent to which Islam must inform every action and word of his life, he has no clear structures of human authority to which he can appeal. And the noise is loud. The technical possibilities of globalization press down on him. Thought from the Indian sub-continent is no longer the privilege of literate *'ulama* in the Yemen, Egypt or Arabia, corresponding like monks in the Middle Ages writing to confrères the other side of Europe. Theological/political debate is on fast forward. While recoiling from the excesses of some of the activists, he may not have the technical arguments to denounce them. Fearing for their own tradition, the *'ulama* are sensitive to the competition they now face from the new radicals. Trimming is not absent.

Furthermore, the sheltered assumption of superiority which in the past Western travellers to the Middle East used to encounter in their Muslim hosts, is now qualified. The assumption is still there, but beset by suspicion and invective from the West, and, in, the

Muslim's view, military invasion. It is axiomatic from all that has been said before, that an attack from outside on this or that Arab state, no matter how secular, is popularly seen as an attack on the Islamic community, a basic interest of the individual Muslim.

Today, knowledge is in spate; a plurality of views undercuts certainties and their emotional securities, but a systematic technique for dealing with contradiction and dissent is lacking. Pluralism is not available. While aspiring to be a collaborative neighbour to the society and culture of the West, he knows that many in the West fear his credo as a slogan for terrorism, or at best in some vague way a legitimation of it. In his religious life, the Muslim Arab surely faces a disturbance of spirits and, with his creed as a comprehensive programme for life, he faces an enigmatic relationship with power.

Chapter 4

Community

As a political term, 'Arab' is familiar to us and it sets the Arab apart from the non-Arab. The term makes sense as a boundary marker. When we cross the boundary and get inside the Arab world, it seems to us an outward-looking word, redolent of the Arab nationalists whose main purpose was to put the Arab world on an equal, but not the same, footing with the outsiders. Inside, strong cultural homogeneity reduces the term almost to mean just 'people'. In fact, deep in Arabia, that was what it did mean until recently, as I have heard it used. 'Take its hood off and let it see the Arabs,' an old falconer told me. I was probably the only non-Arab for hundreds of miles. The falconer just meant, 'see the people' so that the hawk might get used to them. Arab identity is assertive of self and a context of values. It presupposes that everyone knows what it means ('because we are all Arabs'). To reach that meaning, we have no institutions or formal structures to guide us. We have to look at the Arabs as people and see what they mean by themselves.

An Arab friend, marooned in London by a flight cancellation, joins us at home for Christmas Day. All goes well. He is brilliant company, highly amusing; he likes the food; he joins in the conversation. It turns out he is one of those (not so unusual in the Arab world) who are sensitive to the supernatural and he is always aware of the presence of jinns and angels wherever he goes. Our home was fine. He told us, 'No problem, it is well stocked with angels.' But I become aware of an underlying confusion, a question waiting to come out. Our friend wants to know, but is shy to ask, 'where are all the others?' He means the family – the aunts and nephews, grandparents, sisters, brothers and cousins, and their children. Another friend who is with us and not familiar with Arabs, is astonished.

'Could be a bit of a crush ... ' But then he unwittingly goes toe to toe with the problem and continues, 'Anyway ... people like their independence ... and, indeed, their privacy – their own way of doing things.' Our Arab friend looks at me blankly.

There is no word in Arabic for privacy, just a neologism (*khususiyah*). It was coined to explain our own foreign sensitivities, translating expressions like 'privacy laws' and 'privacy agreement'. *Khususiyah* does not contain associations like 'home' (another word for which there is no near Arabic equivalent), and certainly no associations which could capture the thoughts and feelings of Christmas. We were at psychological impasse.

To say that there is no equivalent word in Arabic for privacy is to make an important point and to miss another. This chapter emphasizes the gregariousness of the Arab milieu, but clearly a culture that stresses so much the autonomy of the individual has a layered and deep awareness of individual needs and rights and these are a matter of stringent respect. What we would call a 'private affair' would be called a 'personal affair'. The sense of the personal, and many of the associations which we would call 'private', is very strong. The language used tends to be spatial: 'inner/outer', 'internal/external', 'apparent/concealed'. To make a comment about someone's appearance without a guaranteed atmosphere of intimacy and good humour, is to be offensive. Who can tell how the appearance reflects what is within and why? Similarly, wide ranges of family matters are off limits for casual enquiry. For very many people, and certainly before the new intrusions of religious intolerance, questions of religious observance were personal and, in the absence of what we would call a clergy in Sunni Islam, a matter beyond the proper interest of other people. So the overlap with our conception of privacy exists, but a wider area of individual sanctuary lies beyond. The whole question of the place and role of women in society is linked to this and dealt with in the next chapter. For now, understanding the differences in attitude towards privacy means looking at the social aspect which so strikes the outsider as such a strong characteristic of life among the Arabs.

The Arab, from the moment of his birth, is utterly social. Arabs strongly dislike being alone and typing this I realize that I am unable to recall finding an Arab all alone. There is always somebody else about. Years ago, I helped an Arab friend arrange a visit to Scotland. He had not been to Europe before and I advised him to sit out the several hours' wait for his connecting flight at Glasgow by staying put in the airport. I would not have bothered to give the advice now. When we caught up with him later, he was full of his noisy evening in a street of Glasgow pubs. Dressed in his cloak and bedouin clothes, he had found his way to a pub and had met with a splendid reception. Drinks bought and drinks given, he had worked his way down the street and was full of praise for the friendliness of the Glaswegians – so unlike us and the (very few) English he had met so far in his life. He had arrived in Wyck in a mood of triumph.

Our own ideas of the 'social' imply the 'other', leaving our own privacy and independence, our home, and going out into the world to be with others and others, if we are lucky, with whom we have chosen to be. The context of family diminishes from school onwards and we leave home shortly thereafter. The Arab individual's context is family all the way through. Social means family. A great many live close to other family members throughout their adult lives. Migration and mobility, the pressures to find work are, of course, eroding the validity of this generalization, but anybody who has stood by the Arrivals Gate of a Middle Eastern airport and witnessed the ecstatic scenes as relations are reunited, will know the underlying truth of the matter.

Beyond household and family lies clan as a subdivision of the larger collective, tribe. No one suggests these relationships are all geniality and harmony, but behaviour is effectively kept in order by two constraints: the ever-present dangers lying outside the group and the internal balancing of responsibility within the group.

Attack or criticism from the outside naturally pulls the group together: 'I against my cousin; my cousin and I against the stranger.' Correspondingly, attacks on other groups may be expected to attract a powerful collective response and this proves often to be a deterrent. Leaving the context of the family group means leaving the safety of assured solidarity.

As in our idea of subsidiarity, responsibility is placed as closely as possible to its liability. This limits the foolish assumption that the wider group will rally round to defend individual wrongdoing. These are the ethics which the Arabs have found do work. Practical efficacy proves itself the best standard against which to work out social values and custom.

A problematic and problem-causing value is that of honour. 'Honour,' an Arab saying goes, 'is what people hear about you: your honour is your reputation.' Honour in the Arab world is not only as an expression of the large collective self-esteem which the individual carries within him, though this is important, but is also seen as an expression of the individual's own seeking recognition in the immediate context of household, family and clan. Here, on the face of it, those without clear leadership functions could well be assigned to pale and ill-defined status. How does the individual impose himself on his community when roles are not much variegated?[1] He asserts a sensitivity about respect and sublimates this into the worthier language of the collective.

The sensitivity to insult is very real and hot-blooded. Criticism and threat provoke reactions which can be unexpectedly radical and intense. I have never seen a knife or gun pulled by someone who did not take to being called a 'donkey', but how many times have I heard foreigners warning each other of the extreme danger of using the word? More interestingly, I cannot remember ever hearing an Arab use the word to another's face. They know themselves very well. One alarming incident of threat to honour in which I was involuntarily caught up involved no language at all. I was sitting with a powerful shaikh in a full *majlis* and we were smoking cigarettes. I pulled out a box of matches to light one and the box was empty. The shaikh called across the *majlis* to

---

1 This was a clear feature of traditional tribal life. Now things are changing rapidly as the young take jobs which do distinguish them according to professional or business achievement and this in turn may have long-term implications for the honour code.

somebody to throw me a light. A box came through the air and I caught it. It was empty. The shaikh next to me looked at the man who threw it over, pulled out his revolver and aiming it at the head of the man, pulled back the hammer. It took me a moment to realize this was not in good part, running with the light and happy mood of the *majlis*. Not so the Arabs. They were at once tense and all eyes on the gun. After a very long pause, an elderly and respected man, rose to his feet and walked across the middle of the *majlis*, saying as he went that a lighthearted slip should not spoil a good evening. As he approached the possible line of fire, the shaikh put his gun away and the man next to me on the other side produced a lighter. I was 22, insignificant among their number and a foreigner, but I was the shaikh's own guest. A jab at my ribs was a stab at his face and, to maintain his enormous honour, he chose to react asymmetrically.

A year or so ago, a highly sophisticated and cultivated American friend looked me up in London and told me about his summer holiday in the Lebanon. He had stayed in the village where his family first came from. He was greatly irritated by the chauvinistic flags put up in the street by local gangs of young men and more so by the fact that they appeared to be drawing electricity off the meter of the house where he was staying. 'I got to the point where I took a pistol and went down into the street and confronted them. The electricity scam had to end and the flags come down in ten minutes or else.' He rolled the revolver in the face of the gang leader. Amazingly, he got away with it and got what he wanted. He told me that what had struck him most was the buzz he felt from behaving like this, getting into step with the local way of doing things. I told him the story in the paragraph above and he laughed. Yes, it was not about tents or villas, lifestyles captured in photographs. It was about honour.

We speak of 'face' as a shorthand for honour. Face means person for the Arabs and the inextricability of honour needs no stating. 'May God blacken his face' is an old fashioned but powerful imprecation. A man on the run from another tribe may turn up as an asylum seeker at the tent of a grand shaikh. As a guest he must be given protection for three days, whatever the weather.[2] He can stay on, if the shaikh hears his tale and, as is likely, agrees to protect him. Such a person puts himself 'in the face of shaikh so and so'. Shaikhs defend their face by taking vengeance for any harm coming to a person 'in their face', like for like, or, for really powerful tribes, even more, up to ten times. If being an Arab is a moral cause, being a bedouin is the elemental form of this quest.

Again, a practical consideration may have lain behind the development of another characteristic social virtue, the ancestral elevation of generosity as a primary value. All in the desert are, or potentially are, in need. An ethic of helping and offering hospitality to the stranger will pay back at some point. Furthermore the wherewithal to be generous could not be hoarded among the nomads. Gold in great quantities would be heavy for camels to carry indefinitely, as are other material possessions which serve no needed function. Camels, which used to be the index of wealth in the inner desert where sheep and goats cannot be kept, needed people to look after them and defend them against raiders. Consistent with the imperative to be generous, the leader of a successful raid would share out the gains among his people and lighten his own load.

That was all in the past, until the 1920s and 1930s when stronger central governments put an end to raiding and this form of economic circulation and distribution. The generosity impulse, however, has survived and Arabs who at best, even if they so choose, have only a romantic and notional connection with the bedouin, still uphold the value on account of calling themselves Arabs. The wealth created by oil, mainly in those states with a strong tribal identity and culture, gave renewed momentum to this important value. The oil shaikhs were extremely generous and those who did not cavil at

2 An amusing instance of an expatriate town Arab not being sensitive to this tradition is a comment in Muhammad Sha'ban's *Islamic History AD 600–750 – A New Interpretation* (Cambridge, Cambridge University Press, 1971) when he sympathetically describes the hardships of the population of Iraq after the Arab invasion in the early days of Islam. He says the Arabs 'lived off the fat of the land, the local populations being required to offer hospitality to any passing Arab for at least three days'.

vulgar displays of wealth, assented to this right and proper fidelity to an important Arab virtue. Great shaikhs live in popular history as models of generosity and people tell with pride of how little they were found to own, when they died.

These are great virtues. The Arabs may be hard-headedly pragmatic, but they are by no means utilitarian in philosophy. The requirements of honour are enough justification for their cast of mind and can impose absolute sacrifice. Nonetheless, these virtues can also have instrumental possibilities. They can, even unconsciously, be used to manipulate. The smarminess we sometimes complain about is just charm in the hands of an amateur. But he will be doing his best with a skill set which everyone needs. The giving of honour can pre-empt a dangerous sensitivity in difficult personalities; and the shade-side characteristic of this is a certain tendency to extravagant praise. I was sitting with a shaikh who was receiving guests coming to pay condolences on the death of his brother. Suddenly, in walked the ruler with a retinue. After they had finished greetings and chatting, I was astonished when my friend started praising the ruler for his condescension, consideration and kindness in visiting the humble house of a family in sadness and mourning. 'Who else but the ruler would think of this and then make time to do it, amid his many and high responsibilities?' And so on and so on. I squirmed inwardly, as he went on and on, shouting really so that everyone in the large gathering might hear. It then occurred to me that this proud (and actually quite arrogant) man felt obliged to behave in this way. What I was seeing as some loss of dignity was in fact a stagey performance which surreptitiously magnified the honour done to him and the honour he won by having the apparent humility to speak up about it. More surreptitiously, yet, the ruler did not seem to mind at all. Behind the slow hand movements of deprecation and 'enough', there was a satisfaction that everything was being done as it should be. The ruler wanted to show his own humility by coming to give honour and honour was being received and returned. Need we go on?

Generosity, particularly among the really rich, can be thoughtless and plainly self-seeking. Open-handed hospitality helps control the guests who are made to realize their actual place in the pecking order of life. We all want to honour the guest by being 'at our best', but the sumptuous palaces and series of waiting rooms through which one is processed in visiting the richer governments in Arabia, leave no doubt in the mind of the observant guest but that this is high investment in 'impression management'. Hawking once in the desert abroad with a prince, we had notice that the local secret police chief was going to call at our encampment (and scrounge some gun cartridges). We all, including the prince, scrabbled round to fluff up the cushions, clear the cigarette ends, and make all ready. Our sisters and wives would have been staggered by our speed and efficiency. Then we all sat down again round the fire in serene and elegant poses, hawks on hand and hot glasses of tea in front of us, so that the scene the secret policeman would meet should be as impressive as we could make it and the honour done to him in the eyes of his own minions all the greater. This too contains generosity.

A shaikh once told me that if it did not hurt to give, then it wasn't really giving. When, on another occasion, I saw him making elaborate preparations for the visit to his encampment of an eminent and aged shaikh from another tribe, and he then sat in the dust at the feet of the old guest who was propped up on cushions and carpets, I could hardly tell that this was a cynical move. It was a powerful act of self-abnegation. His slaves, servants and companions were very struck by the gesture, despite his already, and even by local standards, legendary reputation for generosity and hospitality. This was the hard edge of really making an effort. Reputation counts on the moral plane. If you are rich, you have had plenty. Did it not occur to you to give? If you die rich, were you hoarding? Had you no rebuke to the tempting voice of avarice?

What is certain is that Arabs are politically astute in making their calculations about these social moves. They just understand the dynamics and mood of any group or gathering much faster than we do. And this can be true even outside their own context. At a mixed picnic in the sands, an Arab friend told me that one of the foreign women present was pregnant, and that another was having an affair with another man present who was not her husband. I knew nothing of this and in the second case it was a long time before I heard of the same. In the first case, it turned out that the woman had not yet told her husband she was pregnant. She had not yet had time to be sure, as she long after told me. He knew from her skin and unconscious body movements in sitting on the sand. The explanation must lie in the Arab's early and intense schooling in people, being brought up surrounded by large numbers of relations in the household, to say nothing of the wider family. Small children often appear in what we would think of as 'grown-up' occasions. Travellers' photographs from Arabia of shaikhs and princes often show them with a hand resting on the shoulder of a (male) child. The children are present and the politics of relationships and interests are the hazards and opportunities which even the young must learn to navigate. When we factor in fathers who have married more than one wife, the complexities for the children can be imagined.

Anger can be majestic and decisive, but is reckoned to be a vice. It amounts to a breakdown in personal independence and, that prized quality, self-control. Consensus and patience therefore emerge as conditions that all must strive to maintain. The conservativism noted earlier reinforces this steely preference for upholding the good of the group. In religion, communal strife (in Arabic, *fitnah*) is classed as a major evil and the faithful are encouraged by tradition to put up even with an unjust ruler to avoid it.

The overall interests and values of the group need expression. The particular responsibility for this is vested in its leadership. The position of head of household is naturally defined. The head of a family is not necessarily the eldest. Primogeniture is not a recognized principle. The head of a tribe is the man deemed by consent to be the one capable of serving the tribe's interests. The traditional name for the head of a group is *al-kabir*, literally the 'great' or 'big' one. A shaikh leads a tribe. A shaikh is likely to come from a family which has produced shaikhs across many generations. His father may have been the shaikh, but he will by no means necessarily be the eldest son. In a large shaikhly family of a large tribe, senior males will often have the courtesy title of shaikh – and their *kabir* may have the title of *amir*, prince, to put focus on him in the throng of shaikhs.

This is a custom which the ruling families of some of the Gulf states have kept up. But I have heard several young shaikhs say that they hate to be called 'shaikh'. Their veneration for the role and the qualities needed to discharge it do not allow them to arrogate the title to themselves, when they know full well that they are not real shaikhs and even doubt whether they ever could be. 'The (true) shaikh does not know the (other) shaikhs' is an aphorism which catches the linkage between individuality and honour. A shaikh faced with those stronger or more powerful than him is likely to be compromised. Arabian tribes may be surprisingly democratic and egalitarian in spirit, but the human need for a leadership which personifies the aspirations of the community is inevitably present. Members of tribes usually live quite independently of the shaikhs and may hardly ever need them or see them, but, of course, talking up the shaikh talks up the whole tribe – honour again. The psychology of this need for leadership, when transferred to the level of the modern state with its powerful media, gives regimes a powerful emotional hold.

The tribal shaikh stays in place for as long as he is held by popular estimation to be capable of his function. This is to provide judgement and settlement of disputes and to represent the tribe in dealing with outsiders, particularly nowadays with the organs and personalities of government. The ideal, however, which surprises our usual assumptions about the possibly claustrophobic pressures of life in a tribe, is enabling ordinary people and households to live as they wish, managing and coping with changing circumstances, all with the minimum of interference. A tribe though genealogically based remains a form of network and a network is the least organized form of organization which can still be called an organization. There is no formal hierarchy. The only organogram would be one which shows the family tree. This is a guide to likely roles and activities, but not necessarily so.

The role of the shaikh in this informal and flexible association – enabling and empowering the living of life – is the original understanding of *hukm,* usually thought of now in a different political climate, as 'rule'. The product of good *hukm,* or rule, is peace. The agreed means of resolving conflicts allow people to be able to live in harmony. Henry Kissinger commented that a major difficulty for his diplomatic efforts in the Arab-Israeli conflict was that the Syrian President, Hafiz al-Asad, had a different conception of peace from the Israelis. Kissinger was not wrong. The Arab conception of peace is importantly about maintaining these agreed means of settling disputes and about the consequent absence of interference. It is not some idealized future condition. Strife is endemic where there are people and the important thing is to be able to keep this down to a minimal level. Arabs see this as the work of persons, rather than institutions.

The honour of the shaikhly role is often kept in a certain family because it is the family which provides the formation and upbringing necessary to take on this formidable responsibility. A shaikhly friend who had been sent on a management course in America told me that he knew perfectly well what townsmen said about the bedouin, that they were unreliable, unwashed and full of lice. He said that he had, nonetheless, enjoyed the course, but he had not learned much in the sessions about managing people. His family, he said, had bred managers of people for some centuries. Without these skills they would have gone under. He had found the skills on offer at the course, unsophisticated. At home in Arabia, the test is stern. The ceaseless petitions of sycophants, exploiters, the socially and politically ambitious, all in addition to the genuinely needy, make a massive drain on emotional resources and strength. The shaikh only succeeds because he can cope with all this. As a consequence, in maturity he will himself be a formidable person, himself reinforcing the collective inclination to form up behind a great leader. These political gifts are what matter. A shaikh, in the old days, who could meet these requirements but who was not by nature cut out for fighting and raiding or who had become too old, could remain as shaikh (of the door – *shaikh al-bab*) and another could be chosen to lead in war as shaikh (of the saddle – *shaikh al-shidad*). The distinction reveals the sound foundations on which custom has been built: the ability to meet the social needs of the tribe comes first and the narrower criteria of excellence in war come second. In the tribal world, the ability to provide this jurisdiction, this influence which allows others to work out their lives as best they may, is also seen as an attribute of purity of blood, a thoroughbred *noblesse* which does *oblige*. It is important here to remember that that purity is shared by all full members of the tribe. *'Asalah,* purity of both blood and honour, is an informing value of the conceptual infrastructure.

In village, town and city, most will assent to these principles – at least when they are explained, for the ignorance of the desert scene is great. I have often been taken aback by this ignorance. Some are just not interested and have little information about the desert; some, typically when the speaker is scoring high as an 'aspirational Arab', claim a great understanding and assert with animation what I have known simply to be untrue. The divides are deep and never more so than when being used in argument.

People in the settled world, away from the desert and the nomads, label their identity firstly and most importantly, of course, by blood and lineage. Arab names are composed of three elements: personal name, father's name (plus names of grandfathers as desired) and a family name which again expresses blood-line, a region of origin or occupation – e.g. *al-Baghdadi* – the one from Baghdad or *al-Khatib* – the preacher. The instinct for an active expression of group, for all the familiar effects of urbanisation, is nonetheless recognizable. Quarters of cities house Christians, newly urbanized bedouin; and military housing estates are a feature of newer suburbs, recalling in modern idiom the original town plan of the Caliph Mansur's Baghdad. In Amman, Palestinians who came across the Jordan as refugees after the first Arab-Israeli war in 1948, are still found living in clusters, reproducing the patterns they had in the towns they had to abandon in today's Israel. They even elect their own *kabirs – umdahs* who, like mayors, fulfil the same functions as their tribal counterparts in providing sponsorship and guarantee to the authorities for members of the community. They help in settling disputes which people hold are better sorted out privately than with the involvement of officials of the state.

In Jordan, the tribal tradition is never far from the surface. I remember a sophisticated Iraqi woman who had bumped her car, complaining that the police had advised her to take a party of relations and visit the other party at home. This is *Jahah*, the first move in a traditional tribal way of solving disputes. The relations help keep the atmosphere calm by bringing new faces to the discussion. If real trouble is expected, say when a death has occurred, then a well-known shaikh or religious figure may be recruited to lead the delegation. The process, which can be drawn out in difficult cases, ends in an agreement on damages and a *sulh*, or truce, is reached. The problem is over. The Iraqi woman I knew was outraged. All she could see was a primitive procedure which made her homesick for socialist and modern Baghdad, and, of course, as a temporary refugee, she had only a limited number of people on whom she could call for help. The point of the tradition, however, is humane and aims at allowing people to solve their problems for themselves, minimizing the intervention of the authorities.

In ancient cities, traces of the mediaeval guilds remain and associations of traders in the *suqs* uphold the self-help traditions. Major merchant families can trace their origins a long way back and have corresponding prestige and, in some senses, political influence. These, together with eminent members of families with long traditions, for instance of religious or civic service, are the *wujaha*, the notables, an expression which now seems dated, but does capture the way in which Arab communities shape themselves to maintain structures which reflect both the values of equality and of solidarity which come from a much more distant past. A good example of the notables is the Nusaibah family in Jerusalem. When, in 638, Caliph 'Umar arrived in Jerusalem, he told his army that they were not to trespass on the Church of the Holy Sepulchre: he knew his own men – they would want to convert it into a mosque. It was a holy place, he said, and they were to respect it. He gave the keys of the church to one of his generals, al-Nusaibah, and he built his men a mosque on the edge of the church's compound. To this day, the senior member of the al-Nusaibah family locks the church after the Good Friday liturgy and opens it again at midnight on Holy Saturday at the start of the Easter celebrations. Across the centuries, the family, no doubt reinforced with this extraordinary responsibility, has played a leading role in the community of Jerusalem.

The impact of modern government on these traditions is the subject of Chapters 6 and 7, but impact is the sensation. The experience of old ways has still not been replaced by a newer social order which is itself the fruit of successful custom. It is telling that modern, mass-circulation newspapers still feel moved to speak in the name of the *usrah*, the family, of the newspaper staff. The instinct for the personal, rather than the prestige of the institution, remains effective, as, whether with wry comments about the English weather or other simple asides, the staff of the BBC Arabic service so brilliantly showed, year after year, thus tightening the personal link between the diaspora in rainy London and their fellow Arabs across the seas.

The growth of 'Arab quarters' in Western cities, like the district round the Edgware Road in London, reflects this strong social instinct. There the Arab personality is unmistakable; the easy tone of the shops and cafes takes us at once to Beirut, Damascus or Cairo. *Narqilah*s (waterpipes) with their smell of apple- or strawberry-flavoured tobacco, newspapers, coffee cups, tins of Nido, strip fluorescent lighting badly wired across the ceiling, and other familiar signs of the Arab making himself at home, create an atmosphere in which the Middle Eastern tourist, refugee or expatriate can reconnect, despite any differences of Arab nationality. The incomers can merge and be absorbed, yet the defences at the boundaries are well protected, not least by the barrier which Arabic raises against the foreigner. The conundrum is that the culture so centred on hospitality also protects itself by standing in sharp contrast, if not actual conflict, with encircling influences. These, after all, stand outside the value 'system'.

At these watering holes deep in foreign lands, local differences from the region are suspended. The most formidable of these, the gap between the desert and the sown (the settled land where agriculture is possible), is not a source of tension. Without doubt there is an ancient antipathy between the nomad and the settled people of the town and village. Critically, they do not much like seeing marriages arranged across the divide. Years ago, the camels of a hungry tribe passing north to escape the coming heat of summer could devastate crops and reduce farming communities to poverty. Tribal alliances were often arranged to protect the farmers from the nomads' lawlessness. As economic and political conditions have changed, so desert people have devised new strategies and lifestyles to adjust to new circumstances Their relations with settled people remain at the same time collaborative and shot through with an element of tension.[3]

As a foreigner, I have had to listen on one side to much vituperation, complaint and angst about the other side, and vice versa. And yet, of course, the reality, the way ordinary people carry on with their own business, speaks more of a deeper, symbiotic relationship in which differing roles and missions are accepted. In the old days, the bedouin were dependent on the markets in the settlements and cities for those products they could not make for themselves. The townspeople were dependent on the goodwill and company of the bedouin for long-distance journeys. Without the escorts to protect them who would give them a temporary status as guests, they were fair game to marauding tribesmen. The tribesmen brought into town meat, wool, dairy products, which were also needed. The banter concealed mutual dependence and, on the settled side, a recognition, even if grudgingly given, of a moral tradition to which they too would like to assent.

This chapter has concentrated on the root system from the past of much that is still visible and remains characteristic today. The spirit of the collective for the Arabs is a powerful heritage, linking generations through the genealogy system and underpinning both the identities of Arab and Muslim. Its vocabulary is self-consciously ethical and sets high standards for people for whom survival in harsh conditions was an achievement in itself. In contradiction to the

---

3 The way the people of different traditions in the desert and countryside have adapted, is described in William and Fidelity Lancaster's *People, Land and Water in the Arab Middle East* (Amsterdam, Harwood Academic Publishers, 1999). This is a remarkable book, both for its detail and for its sympathetic insight, for those interested in this aspect of change.

cultures of settled peoples, like the Ancient Egyptians, the collective value is woven on the basic values of personal freedom and equality. This pitched individuals, socially, but not necessarily religiously, against the phenomenon of organized political power.

This chapter has not touched on the lives of Arab women. Though Arabic may not have an equivalent word for privacy and our concept of it is foreign to them, there is a domain in Arab social life which is 'private', being opposed to what is public, and that is the domain of the women. It seems prudent to give it its own chapter.

Chapter 5

Women

In 1982, I was posted to our embassy at Belgrade. I set off for a visit to Kosovo. I knew we were getting close to the provincial capital, Pristina, by the way new and high walls became more and more common and obvious, enclosing villas, gardens and even quite simple houses. For me there was a reassuring familiarity in this – I had recently been living in the Middle East. For my Serb travelling companion, the sight was painful and he said so with vehemence. He was in quite a state by the time we got to the outskirts of the city. For him, the walls represented the East, the ineradicable bruise of the Turkish defeat of the Serbs in 1389 at Kosovo Polje, the earlier heartland of the Serbian kingdom, and, today, the walls expressed the fast growing self-confidence of the Albanian Muslim population in the province.

For him, the walls had no happy associations with Damascus, old Cairo or Jedda. For if you get well away from the main streets of these cities, you feel you are in blank corridors between high walls. Small and often insignificant gates and doorways, which are always shut, perhaps lead into unknown secret gardens and stories reaching back across generations, a world of colour and noise, while the street or alley remains neutral, featureless and impersonal.

My first experience of walls around houses in the East was in 1970. I drove down from Oxford to Ankara and on the way had an invitation to look up friends of my parents who had a summer house on the Asian shore of the Bosphorus. We rang in and were asked to come round at once. We had difficulty finding the small door in the long, white and ochre walls of the village. Hot and creased from the journey, we stepped inside and found ourselves in an early evening drinks party, elderly guests seated at small tables in a courtyard running down under trees to the water's edge. Expensive handbags, silk dresses, light laughter and the clink of glasses being handed out by waiters; the two of us were in jeans. We could not have been more embarrassed. As we were brought past the tables to where our hostess was sitting, I noticed that people were speaking not only Turkish, but French. Our hostess addressed us in French and when this did not work, changed to English. Everyone at all the other tables thereupon began to speak English as well. We had moved from the dangerous free-for-all of public space, the roads and streets, traffic and trade, into private space, family and hospitality. This separation between public and private space is the massive distinction between Eastern and Western societies. In the East, half the population should be mainly confined, according to religious precept and tradition, to private space; public space is the sphere of men and men only.

Arabic may not offer a traditional word for private, but the no-go areas in Arab social life are, well, more or less, the half of it. The private space is not just defined by individual choice or individuality. The private space is laid down for society and by society. The language used is very ancient and affirmed, a Muslim should say sanctified, by Koranic injunction and religious use. In Arabic, words from the tri-literal root *HLL* are to do with what is permitted: *halal* meat has been killed in the right ritual way and is permissible as food (i.e. the blood, meaning life, has been drained out of it). Words from the root *HRM* are the direct antithesis to *HLL* and are to do with what is *not* permitted, whether because unpleasant and wrong (as in the Arabic expression *'ya haram'* – 'Oh Shame!') or because what is not permitted is reserved, set aside, perhaps because sacred (as in *al-haram* – the sanctuary of the Ka'abah, the holy house built by Ibrahim at Mecca). The collective for women is *al-Harim*.

This tinkering, tentative way into this chapter reveals my own inhibitions. What has a foreign man to say about Arab women? I have, of course, met many Arab women, but, in the natural way of things in the East, nothing like as many as the men I have met. Encounters have to some extent been privileged, or even risky. In a tent in Arabia, a couple of years after the drinks party on the

Bosphorus, I saw that a bad dust storm was approaching across the desert and became a bit worried about three falcons on their perches at the end of the tent. Beside the tent was a high-walled, stone house where the shaikh's women lived. I, of course, had never been inside the wall. The storm came towards us with astonishing speed and violence and in a moment the tent was dark and at risk. The men held the poles and attended to the guy ropes. I grabbed the hawks and ran them into the house. Suddenly, I was surrounded. Used only to figures in the distance, dressed in black, I was now face to face and surrounded by bright, highly made-up women of a range of ages, dressed in brilliantly colourful long dresses, all noisily amused that I should have burst in upon them. I settled the hawks down and departed. When the shaikh returned in the evening, the story was told over and over again around the fire in the tent to gold-toothed laughter. I was lucky and, as a friendly guest, privileged. When I met some of the women again 30 years later, they still remembered and laughed.

I found none of this shocking. I am old enough to remember when our own women had their own schools and colleges and to remember the very distinctive and special atmosphere they created. Much, of course, has changed in the Arab world in the intervening 30 years, and yet, only the other day, I was shown round a private university for girls in the Gulf and felt the same sense of being an intruder, fixed by glances from veiled faces and black headscarves, as soon as I was shown into a lecture room or library. The situation of women in the Arab world is dynamic, but the season is early spring, first shoots, and not early summer.

If the concept of private space is linked to what is reserved and not permitted, it is also linked to what must be defended. A man's *haram* is what he fights for. With regard to women, the primary danger is deemed to come from males whose passion could cause a breach in the code of honour and the integrity of blood-line. That means any male to whom, if she were not already married, she might be married. This security assessment of Arab sexuality is their own. It may seem far-fetched, but it runs across the centuries, across changes in fashion, culture and social mores which range from the sophisticated, wine-drinking, easy days of episodes at the court of the 'Abbasid caliphs in the Baghdad of a Thousand and One Nights to the neo-puritan conditions of modern Saudi Arabia. Thus a woman is at risk in the presence of men, and, away from immediate family, she should to some extent be veiled. A veil, for these purposes, is what covers the female form, especially her hair which is considered a point of glory in a woman's beauty. The veil, as a covering for the face, is not Koranic and seems to be a custom of supererogation for the extra-observant. Traditional Muslim women do not like being looked at, and as the face is often the first to be noticed, the temptation to cover the face is strong. I took a friend's mother out to lunch at a restaurant in the country. She was dressed in a long black outfit with a black head-dress. Her tribal tradition was not to cover the face with a full veil. Sometimes she held it there with her teeth, giving her a striking look of both determination and apprehension. Whenever we went through a village and someone was close to the car, she drew the scarf across her face. I wondered if this was the training of a lifetime, or whether she was shy to be seen in a car with a foreigner. I asked her. 'I just don't want the beasts looking at me at all!' was her reply. At the restaurant, in a formalized situation where there were unveiled women and other foreigners, she did not veil her face once. In London, her first visit away, in spite of having no English, she made friends in all the shops and super-markets near where she was staying. The idea of being married to any of these strange foreigners would not have entered her head. She felt no risk.

My wife once at a party of women unguardedly asked what heaven would be like for them, seeing that there were promises of attendant virgins for the men. 'My dear,' one replied, 'in my heaven, there will be no men at all.' The question naturally arises in our minds whether women in the Arab world generally see the con-straints of this tradition of protection and reserve as an imposition, or not. While it would be unrealistic to suggest that Arab societies, in their many forms, exist in a state of angst and tension on account of the grievances of the women, it is probably fair to notice that the natural hopes of mothers for a better life for their offspring very largely include greater freedoms and choice for their daughters. They know the hardships they themselves have seen.

One of the reasons for this, in my experience, is that the women, for all the constraints and their consequent lack of experience, have less trouble adjusting to change and modernity than do the men. A friend arrives on his first visit to Europe and is pleased to be photographed in London against the background of Big Ben. He rather sheepishly hands me the shopping list written out by his wife who has never left Arabia. It is very difficult to read (Arabic writing omits short vowels). On consultation with my wife, the letters transliterate names of the main shops in London, like British Home Stores, which are vague to me and where he is to look for the listed items beneath. Another friend arrives on honeymoon with his wife who has also never been out of Arabia. Having changed on the aeroplane, she is dressed *à la mode* and, on setting off into London, with my daughter, makes a beeline for all the latest accessories and styles. She is, to all appearances, indistinguishable from a young woman brought up in London. Staying with my wife with friends in Arabia, we are given a light scratch lunch in the kitchen before going out. Places are set with new Habitat-style cutlery and mugs at the table. A brother comes in and asks why we have to sit at table, 'Why can't we eat as we should?' by which he meant on the floor, in a circle around the food. 'If you want to eat like an animal, you can have a plate of your own on the floor by yourself,' is the from-the-hip sisterly riposte. He joins us at table. Women often assert that they are more down to earth and practical because they have to face the realities of life, like bringing up families. Arab women undoubtedly know which side of the barricade they are on in this discourse.

The Arab Human Development Report, a UNDP publication written by Arab contributors in 2002 for the Arab Fund for Economic and Social Development,[1] states that over the last three decades adult literacy has doubled and women's literacy has trebled, yet women's illiteracy remains at 60 per cent across the population

1 The text of this and later reports can be found at www.rbas.undp.org/ahdr.cfm

of the 22 member states of the Arab League. In the socially more conservative countries, where there may be girls' schools, the girls who get to them have an opportunity to compete with their brothers. If they do well, they can create opportunities for themselves which their parents, even if they are not already supportive of their daughters' ambitions, may find it hard to gainsay. Girls, accordingly, work hard and do strikingly well. In 1997, at the university in al-'Ain in the United Arab Emirates, 82 per cent of students were girls. The impact on their fathers, brothers and husbands of this surge, not just in literacy, but in high competences and expertise is yet to be fully understood. At present, people are doing what at the time seems unarguably the right thing to do – educate the women. This is not the same as being able to foresee, never mind shape, the future. Accommodations will have to be made to include these new women in the public space and cope with the possible deficit which may open up in the home and in the family. In time, the profound changes this will precipitate will become apparent, but from what we have already seen of blood and family, the changes will be running against a deeply conservative grain and therefore likely to take longer than many would like.

In countries where social change has been more explicit, particularly those where revolutions occurred in the 1950s and 1960s, girls' education is longer established but so, it has to be said in most cases, are long-running structural economic preferences in favour of the social sector and government control which have failed to keep pace with fast-rising populations. Unemployment and, at best, the concealed unemployment of hollow jobs, create conditions in which the prejudices can persist against employing women and developing careers for them. Those women who can, by contrast with their sisters outside the region, get beyond jobs in support and service roles, who can build on their educational qualifications by getting access to, and achieving success in, the professions or management, are the lucky ones. Although I have found no statistics to establish this, the impression just remains that employment is still less than common for the married woman with children.

The demands of family life and the expectations of husbands still favour women finding their fulfilment in the home. Needless to say, the burden of work there is enormous. Labour-saving accessories and convenience foods are not the norm, though, in the former case, this is not a matter of prejudice, more likely of cost. Some tribal friends during a discussion of yoghurt which is traditionally made by swinging it in a goatskin, said they had given all that up, once they had discovered that a basic washing machine could do it just as well – the rhythmic turning of the barrel had just the right effect. When I intervened to ask what this did for the next load of clothes, they looked at me as though I was mad. 'That goes in the other machine, Mark … '

Traditional cooking, itself a matter of prestige and therefore touching on honour, is labour intensive. Households are large and families even bigger. Fortunate are those young couples who, when they marry, can afford a home of their own. The young wife is often an incomer at the parental home and an immediate subordinate to a mother-in-law or sister-in-law; she has to join a team with a lot of management work to do and a lot of hard labour. The pressures to conform and adjust to the responsibilities of the married woman will be intense.

It is therefore little wonder that the situation of Arab women, their rights and opportunities, are a matter of great interest outside the Arab world and that, inside the Arab world, the communications possibilities of globalization have increased not only the level of talk, but also of feminist attitudes. I remember an elderly but eminent Palestinian giving a seminar on the prospects for change in Palestine. He chose to build his talk around an acute insight that the Palestinian administration was chronically and dangerously disorganized – they just could not, he said, identify workable social objectives and deliver on them. In answer to a question about the role of women, he noted that women had a vital role to play in the building of a new society. In his view, most Arab men were write-offs by the time they reached adolescence. They were spoilt by their fathers and brothers and waited on by their sisters and mothers. The result was men who had no comprehension of organization, nor any sense of responsibility for good administration. The vital mission was to raise a generation of Palestinian men who could stand on their own two feet. A young woman in a white headscarf challenged this and asked why the speaker should concentrate on women's reproductive functions. This was in the UK, but nonetheless a cameo of a clash, not just of outlook but also of willpowers, which is unlikely to abate in our lifetimes.

A quick check on the Internet for 'American Women' in April 2005 produced 101 million entries, for 'English Women' 48.4 million, for 'Western Women' 28.2 million, for 'European Women' 27.5 million and for 'Arab Women' 9.4 million. Considering that the UNDP's Arab Human Development Report places the Arab world at the bottom of the world's seven regions for access to information and computer technology (below sub-Saharan Africa), this represents a considerable, and probably fast-rising, volume of opinion. A few and random selections from the Arab Women entries revealed an unsurprising range of straight talking – chat rooms discussing whether the boys want a mother, a wife or a lover (with heavy voting going to the first and last); organizations committed to tracking and improving women's rights; and instructions, in a site for Western women in the Arab world, on how to be a good wife and a good husband. This last turned out to be not just a self-help opportunity for foreign women, but also an Islamic evangelical site offering advice on how women should always make themselves 'beautiful and sweet smelling'; and, for their husbands, on not letting a wife go outside for long periods, on being sure to get her up in the last third of the night for prayers, and on mild physical chastisement. The force of tradition is as agile in mastering the new technology as the get-ahead new thinkers. Arab women are not in a one way street towards what we might recognize as emancipation. The counter-flow is not weak.

Two subtle elements contribute to this counter-flow. Firstly, Arab men, perhaps like men in southern Europe, pay far more attention to their mothers than do those in the colder north. A saying of the Prophet on personal obligations and priorities runs, 'Your mother, then your mother, and then your mother.' This filial devotion is notable and not a myth. And the mothers I have met deserve it all.

Well, most of them do – the same pressures and hardships which in large families and clans make the leaders into remarkably strong and powerful personalities, have a corresponding burnishing effect on the women. Arab society is patrilineal, but some of the senior women are massively impressive. The perspectives for the young wife, however, are challenging, as is the social demand that she quickly produce a son. For the first birth marks, in subliminal way, the end of probation. The birth of a son confirms her status as a success in the marriage: the arrival of a daughter can be an amber light. And delighted though new fathers may be with their baby girls, there just is a difference when they are presented with a new son. Their blood-line is thus secured. I remember a young man expressing how much the new generation means to the wider family. He was complaining that his brother and new sister-in-law had not yet produced children. 'We must have more children. We need them.'

Secondly, the conventional tone of young love life is romantic. Airbrushed colour picture postcards of a drippy young man watching his sweetheart pull petals off a rose; the 'he loves me, he loves me not' soliloquies in Egyptian soap operas; the demure but coquettish behaviour of young Arab women – all voice the same tone of suppressed frankness, of sentimental idealization and an indiscriminate sublimation of physical expression. And this romantic culture goes back. There are good grounds for believing that the mediaeval tradition of courtly love was imported from the Arabs and Saracens via the crusades and the sophisticated society of Muslim Spain. Although it is now no longer living history, the memory is strong of accounts of a beautiful girl being put into the howdah on a camel's back during a major set-to battle. The young braves of the tribe would then gather round the camel to defend her, as infantrymen would defend the colours in a European army. This was a familiar practice until vehicles transformed tribal raiding into blood-baths and gave the long arm of central governments an immediate and local punch. The battle-cries of tribes often included '(I am) The Brother of 'Alia', or some other girl's name, and these soubriquets became a way of referring to a tribe – each by its own

'Brother of so-and-so' variant. As noted earlier, the Arabs are well aware that a love match trumps an arranged marriage contract. The paradox of this romantic mood in a world where so many women get a seriously raw deal, can only be observed, but it touches on a theme of this book, an aspirational temper, a vision of life which explains itself to itself in fiercely ideal language. As one might expect, the practice is another matter.

Contemporary heroines are not hard to find, but their stories may not have been loudly enough proclaimed. A Saudi friend of mine, like a good many others, drove up to Kuwait behind the military column which liberated the city from the Iraqis in 1991. He was taking emergency supplies to friends. He parked by the seashore to look at the scene. He became aware of a young woman looking into the back of his pick-up. She was eyeing the packs of Coca-Cola stacked up in the back. 'Oh, I've not had one of those since last August … Can I have one?' They got into conversation and she spoke of a girlfriend who had disappeared. She had been part of a resistance group and had been picked up by the Iraqis. From her prison she had managed to send out tiny pieces of paper on which she had written the car numbers of those cars she then realized had been part of the Iraqi surveillance operation against them. This had saved others later. She was never heard of again.

The women of Kuwait showed extraordinary courage and toughness during the occupation. Those who had been unable to escape at the start of the invasion knuckled down to keeping their communities afloat in a way that astonished the cynics more used to the apathy of peacetime and 'room service' conditions in Kuwait. The women organized rubbish collection and disposal, help-lines and supply-lines. They played their part in the resistance and information networks that stayed in touch with the Kuwaitis in exile. In a BBC documentary about the British Special Operations Executive (SOE), tasked by Churchill with 'setting Europe alight' in the Second World War, the ex-Director of SOE commented in interview that he had seen in young women a 'quality of courage he had very rarely seen in men'. He would not have been surprised, as many others were, by the Kuwaiti women.

The Kuwaiti episode is one example. Across the region, political events put a hidden pressure on the women who have to maintain the dailiness of family life and the upbringing of the young. Palestinian women living under occupation and the shadow of collective punishments, living in the diaspora of exile and refugee camps, Iraqi women during the long war with Iran and the coalition attacks since, Algerians with their years of civil stress and Lebanese with their still recent civil war, these and others have silent stories. Because we meet so little with them, we have little idea how to decode their experience and its influence on their societies. The domestic effect of migrant labour, mainly from the populous north to the oil-rich south and east, but also northwards from the Yemen, is an effect that many might have chosen to avoid, if they could have, once they have tasted it.

So the demureness of the (slimming) black outfits, the courtly reserve and polite light laughter are only, of course, part of the story, greatly though they contribute to impression management. The daughter of a friend whose family was at one time engaged in smuggling, once told me of her suspicion one dark night when she was unaccountably alone in the tent, that someone was interfering with a large truck parked up outside and containing contraband. 'What did you do?' I asked with round eyes. Hers narrowed. 'I fired half a clip from a Kalashnikov over the back of the truck. I fired the other half of the clip high in the direction I thought somebody was running, and went back into the tent.' Knowing both the life she led, and her husband and father, I wondered later why I should have found the story remarkable. If I am honest, it was the paradox of gentle appearance and such decisive action.

An Arab woman, on marriage, does not take her husband's name, save on invitations sent out by foreigners. She remains strongly the daughter of her father and her own family will be important connections for her children. If divorced, she returns to her father's house. Much of the dowry she receives is still traditionally in gold and jewels and these are inalienably hers. They are a reserve for use in the event of an emergency, like the early death of her husband, or a divorce. Women have powerful stature as vessels of family and blood-line honour. In the home, in many cases, they rule. The psychological shift through which the men pass when they move from the *majlis* where guests and outsiders are received, to the women's quarters, is remarkable (but rare) to see as an outsider. Much, however, is spoken about this. The women are extremely well informed. They have the background brief for every occasion and eventuality. The women are strong, not least because they need to be. And while they uphold the social and family system, they seem to have fewer illusions about it than do their menfolk. The romantic, misty-eyed phase seems to clear up quite soon in married life, while for the men it settles in – perhaps until they have adolescent daughters to get at them. The women may live in a real seclusion (the ancient caravan town of Ghadames in western Libya was constructed so that women can pass from house to house to visit neighbours via bridges across the rooftops, rather than descend into the street), but they live on the edge. Honour killings are falling out of fashion, a bit, and are even being legislated against, as in Jordan, but they are not a thing of the past. Death can still be the penalty for a transgression.

A group of friends was recently discussing a case which had ended with the killer's execution. He had returned home unexpectedly to find his wife and his best friend in bed. He had gone back out to his car, taken his revolver from the glove compartment and returned to the house. He shot both his wife and her lover. The judge had told him that if he had had the gun with him and had shot the pair on sight, then he would have only been guilty of a crime of passion. In fact, he had walked to the car and back and therefore had time to know what he had in mind. His crime was premeditated and therefore he would have to be killed. My friends deliberated on this story from many angles, many of them tolerant and liberal. They said they knew their own natures and wondered if the distance to the car and back allowed enough time for an Arab in these circumstances to come to his senses. Should he have killed his wife too? The talk went round and on. Then one intervened, 'You know, if the wife was his uncle's daughter (as would have been very likely), then he had to kill her. He had no choice.' Everyone quickly agreed. The man next to me lent sideways and quietly explained, 'Then it's blood and it's honour.'

The outsider is left silent in thought at the interior and hidden dramas that must afflict the lives, or at least the imaginations, of many Arab women.

Chapter 6

The Problem of Power

Ultimately, political questions are rooted in the problem of power. The human desire to exercise power, to control others around us, presents itself as a hard fact. Then another fact stands in the face of this: that we insist on defending ourselves and own interests. We resist the assertion of power. This contradiction has to be resolved, whether it concerns groups or individuals. Societies limit power in a variety of ways: they limit it in some formalized adversarial competition; or they collectivize it by bringing in others who are not at first involved, as in elections and law courts. They dilute the elements of conflict by engaging wider concerns and interests. They cleave to questions of legitimacy. For the problem of power is always how to contain it.

Whatever the means chosen to restrain power, those who are most drawn to power usually re-emerge in the key positions. Their dealings with each other are politics and because these people are powerful, others have to deal with them politically as well. Scale obviously makes all these matters more difficult. It should not, however, follow that the techniques developed by smaller communities have in some way less depth. Larger societies are obviously powerful. Their leaders cut larger figures, but they are not therefore necessarily more right about how best to handle power, the fundamental question with which even the smallest groups are struggling.

In his book, *The Shield of Achilles*,[1] Philip Bobbitt outlines the historical development of the idea of the nation in our own world. His description illuminates our own assumptions about power and

1 London, Penguin, 2002.

the political community. His work reminds us what a transfer of understanding we have to make to reach the factors which drive political ideas in the Arab world.

Bobbitt argues that three drivers have governed the course of our story. The first is law which expresses and enforces the political requirement for legitimacy and ultimately the sovereignty of rule. The second is strategy, particularly in the traditional military sense of rulers' means of identifying and dealing with both threat and goals. The third is history – that narrative which explains and defines both our today and our hopes for the future. History, like law, is a chosen way of supplying and reinforcing legitimacy. It records those parts that have mattered to those able to choose and write their own stories.

Bobbitt takes a large view of the past to demonstrate how princes gave way to princely states. The princes increasingly faced the need to enlarge both their military forces and the bureaucracies to administer them. They needed these to cope with the threat from new military technologies (especially those relevant to siege operations). He demonstrates how those new bureaucratic structures and power centres led to state functions of the kind we can recognize today and which transcended the fortunes of individual rulers. From there, he traces the emergence of kingly states: how new thinking about the king's sovereignty enhanced the authority of the structures of the state at the expense of the authority of the king. Sovereignty also found its limitations defined territorially and this brought into being the notion of a geographical political unit, the 'territorial state'.

From 1776 to 1914, Bobbitt sees a transformation from 'state nations' in which legitimacy still derived from above, to 'nation states' in which the state's legitimacy derived from its ability to provide the people with defence and public goods, like rudimentary welfare and education.

At the end of the twentieth century, Bobbitt's sense of the great conflicts of the 'modern era', the First and Second World Wars and the ensuing Cold War, is of a continuum of conflict, a Long War between three political projects, themselves engendered by the problems of the nation state and the vying for control of the nation state. These three projects were fascism, state socialism and parliamentary democracy. From this review and the apparent victory of the last of these, parliamentary democracy, Bobbitt sees the emerging possibilities for what he terms the 'Market-State'. He argues that strategy in a post-détente world characterized by the proliferation of weapons of mass destruction and a new terrorism which threatens potentially strategic damage, must be about to change; that law as a technique for controlling international disputes (e.g. through the UN and world courts) has in important senses failed; and that the story of state provision of welfare and securing the public interest shows that the state can no longer sustain the costs of meeting public expectations. Health, transport, education and many other services which people, for more than half a century, have expected governments to provide, are now beyond reasonable government budgets, or at least what the people are likely to accept as fair taxes to pay for them. So Bobbit argues that the compact between government and people which underpins legitimacy, must change. He sees politicians moving in the direction of a new project – offering new and greater opportunities for individual self-betterment and choice – as their means of capturing public support and performing against public expectations.

Also from an avowedly Western standpoint, Roger Scruton's *The West and the Rest*[2] examines the significance of law as precedent and common usage in the West. He compares it with adherence to law as an aspect of divine revelation in the Islamic world. He considers the history of the constraints imposed by geography, the limits of political power and their effect on jurisdiction – and thus the meaning of law itself. A writ, he observes, runs as far as it can be enforced and no further. Taking the example of England's experience, he shows how an island state can more quickly develop its own legal tradition of precedent, common law and nationhood because the physical limits of its society, and so the political limits, are so clear.

2 London, Continuum, 2003.

Geography is important to the Arab story. Arabia was the forge in which the Arab identity was wrought and the place of the revelation which preserved the centrality of Arabia in the Islamic story. The surrounding geography presented the challenges and influences that created the tensions which make up so much of that story. It deserves a moment's consideration.

The geographical factor is immediately obvious to the visitor to the Middle East: water in sufficient quantities to support agriculture is hard enough to find and the map quickly shows where agriculture was rich enough to support the growth of towns and cities. This dependency of the city on its hinterland of food production is less obvious to us living in temperate climates. In the Arab world, vividly, water, like blood, is life and the existence of a city means the superabundance of it. The vanishing of ancient cities like Gerrha on the Persian Gulf or Saba in the Yemen speaks of a change in the availability of water. Leptis Magna in Libya collapsed as a viable Roman city when the inhabitants found the city's water supply had become polluted. They simply had to move out.

Strategic locations are first and foremost places with good water. Thus Egypt, Herodotus noted, is 'the gift of the Nile'. The cities of Mesopotamia, between the Tigris and Euphrates, have ancient histories and civilizations. Damascus is traditionally known as the oldest continuously inhabited city on earth. It lives on a water table supplied by the mountains of the anti-Lebanon, and the river Baradah which flows through it. As importantly, the surrounding countryside is rich and yields a surplus which supplies the needs of the city and allows the farmers to diversify and use the city as a market.

Within these delicate eco-systems a local personality develops. *Bilad al-Sham* ('the country round Damascus') historically extends from Aleppo to Ma'an in southern Jordan. It is a distinctive cultural zone which reaches across today's national borders, but contains many sub-sets of local tradition which merge with, or are connected to, elements further afield. Damascus is its magnificent hub. We think of Iraq as being better defined because its contemporary boundaries seem coherent, but nonetheless it contains a variety of traditions – Persian, Arab, Kurdish, Turkish and other elements stemming in some cases from way outside its own region, echoes of the 'Abbasid empire's reach into Central Asia. The Tigris and Euphrates allowed a more diverse society to develop and the political geography was consequently always much less stable. While Damascus always dominated *Bilad al-Sham*, Iraq generated different great cities which rose and declined as political fortunes shifted. Babylon is now archaeology; Nineveh is supplanted by its successor, Mosul; Baghdad was founded by the Arabs in 760, but declined when the irrigation system in Mesopotamia was damaged by civil war in the Arab empire. In 1253, the Mongols overran it and ploughed it with salt. By the late nineteenth century, Baghdad was a depressed and marginalized administrative outpost in an Ottoman province. Iraq's life-blood, however, remains its great rivers. The main towns of the Kurdish hinterland in turn depend on rivers like the Zab. These draw from the mountains of Kurdistan and allow a different and non-Arab society to survive. The unfortunate Kurds have a saying that they have 'No friends but the mountains'.

These northern territories were not significantly Arab until the expansion of Islam from Arabia. Iraq had its own Sumerian and Assyrian civilizations until it was dominated by the Persian empire. The ancient language of Syria, always uneasy between the influence of Persians, Egyptians, Romans and Byzantines, was Aramaic – one of the family of Semitic languages and a great cultural and commercial medium going back into prehistoric times. The Syrians were the first non-Arabs to be overrun by the Muslim armies.

Settlements in Arabia show the same pattern of dependence on water. In the past, the oasis towns of today's Saudi Arabia, the coastal towns along the Gulf and Red Sea were, in their own way, microcosms of the larger societies around the northern cities. They were market towns and coastal trading stations which, even though in much smaller degree, gave personality to their regions. The Yemen, steep and mountainous, was able to support a more crowded village culture. Geographically, it seems a southern counterpoint to the Kurds in the far north. While unmistakably Arab, the Yemen has developed a strong local personality which distinguishes it from the interior of the peninsula.

The lines of communication between these regions, zones and settlements, though often sea lanes connecting the Arabs of the peninsula to Iran, India and Africa, were also trade routes which passed through long marches of desert. The desert was the scene of quite another eco-system. Its nomadic inhabitants, deeply conservative in their unchanging circumstances, were proud and avowedly independent. Their wide-ranging and confident desert culture was a powerful influence. Much is often made of the contrast and tension between the desert and the people of the villages and towns. Their relationships, however, were also greatly coloured by what they had in common, their many interdependences. The great trading caravans connecting the Hijaz with Damascus needed the laissez-passer of the nomads through whose stamping grounds the caravans passed. The spread of the Arabs across the peninsula since prehistoric times is usually attributed to nomadic expansion and then settling as groups came on richer land they could defend. Thus for many apparently settled people, nomadic forebears were part of the family or clan story. The values were inherited.

The desert reaches a long way north and divides Iraq from Syria, Egypt from Palestine. Nomads were therefore present in the mosaic of cultures in the north. But they knew where they came from and many maintained their continuities and connections with other Arab tribes in the south. Just beyond the frontiers of the villages on the edge of the lands that had enough water to support settled life, the 'conceptual infrastructure' of the desert, described in Chapter 2, was in operation. The language of this nomadic conceptual infrastructure was Arabic.

Where this Arabian world encountered the strong neighbouring cultures of Persia, Byzantium and Egypt, complex interactions and mutations occurred. The pre-Islamic Arabs in contact with these powerful civilizations were very self-conscious and self-assertive about their own culture. The early references to them, tracked by Robert Hoyland,[3] speak of the same unmistakable, independent character that we recognize today. Hoyland follows the Arabs'

3 See Hoyland, *op. cit.*

promotion of their language in the two centuries before the Prophet. The Koran itself has eight emphatic references to its being in Arabic. Arabic poetry raised a distinctive voice that reverberated across desert, village and town. Among its functions at religious feasts and commercial fairs was its influence in confirming a common macro culture across the varying micro cultures of Arabia.

For these tribal Arabs, the idea of rule was expressed by *hukm*, a word which captures wisdom, judgement, arbitration. In their tribal society, the task of the leader was settling disputes, representing the group outside (and often this would mean being invited in to settle disputes in other tribes), and also, among the nomads, leading the tribe in its raids and wars against other tribes. The purpose was to defend in each community the conditions in which people could lead their lives according to their own wishes, according to the basic principles of personal independence and personal equality in tribal law. This 'live and let live' idea was what worked. Seen from a distance, it must have been some compensation for the nomads' daily confrontation with the trials and hardship of the desert life. The life of the nomads, no strangers to thirst and starvation, was materially precarious. There is no need to imagine that the practice of *hukm* was always successful. Personality and ambition created some shaikhs and leaders who were a burden to their people. But for the tribesmen, dignity and reputation were considerably up to the individual's own success in making the right decisions. And for those who survived long enough, the dignity of age was a reward for a life long lived. The thematic idea, brought down to us by tradition and the acclaim of successive generations, was clear: leadership was a role which was not only about authority, but also service. The idea of being an anonymous and passive object in the face of power was absent.

Within this strongly tribal society, politics thus had a bias towards the conciliar and consensual. Absolute rule was not the tradition. Consonant with the idea of the exercise of power as service, political power was best expressed in influence. And what happened to this tradition, as the early Islamic conquests brought it into contact with other cultures and new political problems, was of profound significance for the Arabs' experience of power thereafter and until today.

The Prophet's removal from Mecca to Medina in 622, the *Hijrah* and the start of the Islamic calendar, marked the beginning of a self-ruling community which was self-consciously Muslim. The expansion of the Muslim community from Medina was rapid. Harnessing the enthusiasm and mobility of the tribes, it quickly reached out towards Oman and the Persian Gulf and up into the territories of Syria and Iraq. This was a religious expansion, conferring a new, really we should say an additional, identity through conversion. But the vectors were intensely Arab. The converted tribesmen were nonetheless independently minded for their new beliefs and were by no means easy to control. The pragmatic and consensual style of leadership shown by the early caliphs in Medina was impressive. They were accustomed to this tribal temper and had to work with it. They did not grow the autocratic overtones associated with their eventual successors, the 'Abbasids. The caliph was simply the successor of the Prophet as leader of the community. Arab tradition made no provision for absolute rule and command, not even for hierarchies of command beyond blood relationships. Consultation, advice and leadership on agreed aims were the task of the *amir* among his own people, even if the conquered peoples of the north were inclined to see in him a monarchical figure of the kind they already were familiar with at home.

The transition from community to kingdom began with the Umayyad dynasty which based itself at Damascus and ruled from 661 to 750.[4] Conquests in Egypt, North Africa, Palestine and to the east put enormous wealth at the disposal of the new Muslim rulers. More significantly for political developments, they also acquired local bureaucratic infrastructures, which were hierarchical and more sophisticated than anything they had needed in the Hijaz or Arabia. These resources, both human and material, must have helped the caliph become, as he did, a more potent and decisive figure.

The Arabian temperament, though, was not yet wholly lain aside.

---

4 The first Umayyad caliph was Mu'awiyah, the great grandson of Umayyah, the cousin of the Prophet's grandfather. He had been posted to Syria as Muslim governor at Damascus in 641.

At Damascus, Muʿawiyah, the first Umayyad caliph and the first Islamic ruler to order executions on political grounds,[5] is still proverbial for his caution in handling others. *Shaʿrat Muʿawiyah*, the hair of Muʿawiyah, refers to the strand of hair which he used to say connected him with his political collaborators. If one pulled away, Muʿawiyah would move towards him; and if he moved closer, then Muʿawiyah, very gently, would pull back. Muʿawiyah would not let the hair break. This expression is still common today to capture the wisdom of consensus and flexibility in political dealings.

In sum, the first caliphs operated within the tradition of leadership within the group. The military failure of the fourth caliph, ʿAli, was a defeat for the assertion that the leadership should be passed down the line of the Prophet's descendants through his daughter, Fatimah. Instead, the leadership passed to another part of the Prophet's family which then seized the opportunity of ʿAli's murder and established itself as a dynasty in Damascus. The move out of Arabia led to enormous economic and cultural change as the Arabs enjoyed the fruits of their conquests. These changes accelerated and deepened when the caliphate passed to another dynasty, the ʿAbbasids. Early along the way, the nature of leadership changed. Where we are to place the exact reasons for this, between economics, realpolitik or the perceived requirements of the religious community, must depend on personal standpoint, but the outcome was clear enough: power headed for the absolute and was able to present this as no departure from religious good practice. The new dynasty saw a need to incorporate the Arab tradition into the establishment culture and did so – though, again, we cannot strictly determine whether they did so for religious or other motives. But the power of the new multifaceted culture at Baghdad did not allow this Arab renaissance to include a revival of the Arab political style at the centre of power.

5 Muʿawiyah ordered the execution of Hujr bin ʿUdai al-Kindi and six others. Hujr was a Yemeni tribesman who supported the cause of ʿAli and was a leading figure in the new community of conquest in Kufa in southern Iraq. In Kufa, disputes among the conquering tribes were proving a force for instability and Muʿawiyah decided to take drastic action to stop them. See Tabari's History for the year 51 AH and Shaʿban, *op. cit.* p. 89, fn.

And in so far as absolute power was not self-consciously placed at the service of religion, it became personalized. This appears to have reinforced the dynastic arguments.

In 750, The 'Abbasid revolution overthrew the Umayyads. The shifting of the centre of power to Iraq magnified the political changes already in train. As had Egypt, Iraq not only offered great wealth on account of the highly developed irrigation systems, but also the competences to operate them. These structures and capacities of power were new to the Arabs. They enabled the maintenance of near-permanent garrisons of troops. And when the armies conquered yet more, the new territories could supply more soldiers. Thus the Persians from Khurasan in today's Iran became a valuable support to power. As foreigners with a strong culture of their own, they had no problem with keeping order among the Arabs. The ancient antipathy between Indo-European Persians and Semitic Arabs was already well established. Their interest was to do the bidding of the caliph who paid them. The ruler, the 'commander of the faithful', found himself in a categorically different order of role. Whatever his instincts to behave according to his own tradition and to promote that tradition as part of the new ideology of the state, the requirements and probably the lures of power led him deeper and deeper in new directions.

Once the new power centre of the Muslim community had been established at Baghdad, the encircling foreign influences made themselves yet more and more felt. The consequences for the Islamic world, the achievements of what became a remarkable and brilliant culture, were far-reaching. Europe was enhanced by the intellectual challenge and stimulus of mediaeval Islam. But the political costs were significant. Foreigners from Iran and Central Asia were drawn into the new centre of affairs through conquest and the economic and political attractions of the new city and capital. While the Umayyads had appeared to have a relaxed attitude to local culture,[6]

---

6 Witness the mosaic and frescoed illustrations on the walls of their desert hunting lodges – scenes of hot baths and nymphs, much more evocative of the Mediterranean than Arabia – as can be seen, for instance, at Qasr al-'Amrah in Jordan.

the caliph at Baghdad and his men of religion perhaps saw the incremental effect of cultural dilution and therefore a possible threat to the power they still held for themselves in Arab hands. And the physical terminus of faith remained in Arabia. The *Ka'bah* at Mecca was the place of pilgrimage and the direction of prayer for the whole Muslim world.

At this distance, we cannot fully tell the caliph's motives. In a region where probably only a minority had Arabic as a mother tongue, official concerns may have included the purity of the religious tradition – upholding the Arabic transmission of revelation – and the non-Arab Muslims' ability to master its linguistic difficulties; their economic and power interests – and this would have included defending Arabic as the language of power and trade; or an external concern to maintain good relations with the Arab tribes who had had such military significance during the conquests. Furthermore, the nomadic Arab tribesmen who had not settled, but stayed in the desert, by dint of their yen for raiding, would have been able to keep themselves on the caliph's dance card because they could threaten his trade routes and he relied on an independent intelligence system which used the camel post for communications. Like racing pigeons to hawks, the camel postmen would have been easy enough prey to the bedouin, had the tribes not been kept sweet. The city was powerful, but not wholly independent of the desert. It could only really secure the roads when marching out with large armies. Punitive raids against the tribes would have had limited effect. The bedouin were adept at disappearing into the inner desert where infantry and troops of horsemen could not follow them.

Whatever the motives, it is clear that the 'Abbasids cultivated and promoted their Arab background. They encouraged research into original and untainted forms of Arabic. This meant the oral tradition, the language of the tribes, unadulterated by neologisms and idiom from the newly acquired territories in the north. Poetry from the desert tribes was collected and linguistically analysed by the learned. Grammars and text books were produced to explicate this and the language of the Koran. And with the medium came the message. The indoor men of letters in the cities gave the erstwhile despised and out-of-doors bedouin a new vogue. The virtues and traditions of the Arabs were extolled.

Despite the considerable numbers of Arabs who moved north as soldiers in the army and others who were settled in and around Baghdad, Basrah or Kufa as beneficiaries of the new regime, the source of this Arabian inspiration remained largely 'off shore', in the desert. As a result, the model remained 'out there', it was not interiorized. The aspirational character of the new community had yet another horizon, in addition to that of religion, for which to long. The work on the Arab theme was done by the city dwellers and some of the great names in this project were not even Arab. Siba-wayh, the author of the first Arabic grammar and who died in 796, was a Persian, as was Abu al-Faraj al-Isfahani, the collector of *The Book of Songs*, 25 volumes of Arab poetry, songs, legend, anecdote and history.

Meanwhile, the authority of the 'commander of the faithful' became more absolute.[7] Court life and politics supplied the ener-vating climate for greater personalization of authority. The foreign cultures inured at that time to despotic imperial rule were absorbed into the caliph's environment. His capacity to see that he had his own way was massively empowered by civil servants and profes-sional soldiers. But family remained the channel through which power was to be passed. The 'Abbasids were a dynasty – 37 of them reigned between 750 and 1258 – and the opportunities for intrigue and the manipulation of the succession played into the hands of the courtiers and power brokers who ran the administration and commanded the troops in the field. These from an early stage were significantly Asian in origin and not part of the Arab family elite or religious establishment biased towards the Arab heritage. At the summit, power merged with family, in the name of faith.

What the Arabs of the empire thought about this must have depended on their ability to square their experience of the 'Abbasids with their own beliefs. Where there was congruence, or some

---

7 An accessible and readable account of this world is given by Hugh Kennedy in his *The Court of the Caliphs* (London, Weidenfeld & Nicolson, 2004).

personal advantage, the new face of power must have proved acceptable. Where it did not, some alienation and recourse back into the heartland of family would have been the alternative. The fast-nesses of family life remained a retreat and a stronghold in society. The situation of the women would have supported this. And that has not greatly changed until our own day. Importantly for our understanding of the contemporary political scene, the self-confident and independently minded Arab mindset has not greatly changed either.

We cannot accurately date the weakening of 'Abbasid control in Arabia in a wider sense than just securing access for the pilgrimage, but it would have been well before their own demise in 1258. From that point, the heartland of Arab society, the conceptual infra-structure, remained outside central government's sure control until the 1930s when governments could use vehicles, air and superior fire-power to subdue dissident or nonconformist tribesmen.[8] This recent technological development and the greater interest of states in the affairs of the desert also broke the economic activity of raiding. The tribes became more and more dependent on transactions with the villages and towns and those who ruled them. The attitudes and values, however, were not eliminated. Echoes from what seems a deep past still reverberate. Arab identity and belief, family and power still form a diamond shape of tensions which frames the political dilemmas of our new century. Law, history and strategy, the themes of our world, are by no means absent – history, in particular, has a special resonance in a region so attached to its past. But they are not the key themes in the Middle East.

For the Arabs, in history and now, the experience of state power has been an experience of loss and coexistence with the absolute. And coexistence with absolute power has not erased the awareness of their own social traditions. In modern times, the failure to make

8 In 1976 Glubb Pasha told me of some of the last raids and military encounters with the tribes in eastern Jordan, how even the most warlike saw the folly of vehicle borne charges with machine guns – the casualties and therefore the costs to the tribe were just too great. See also William Lancaster's *The Rualla bedouin Today* (Cambridge, Cambridge University Press, 1981), pp. 142–45.

participatory politics work has left open the divide between ruler and ruled. Power has not been contained by society at large. In spite of a good deal of populist rhetoric in the middle of the twentieth century, power has quickly reverted to its historical type. It has stood opposite society; and society has had to adjust to minimize the threat latent in this polarity.

The irony is that where there are no formal politics, everything is political. The alertness of the Arabs to the politics of the family, clan and tribe, the street and the market, has made them strikingly agile and astute in dealing with the interests of the powerful. This has not, however, helped them work out the kind of solutions that would appeal to us with our love of speculative and innovative political thought. The official politics of the Arab states are therefore intense, but they are not formalized. They tend to deal with power indirectly and in coded language. The interior life of the regime is 'private business'.

Open discussion, therefore, of what to do about the problem of power has been limited. Outside the system, there has, of course, been discussion, but not in dialogue with power – hence the high incidence of coups d'état in the last half-century. The population's role was but a walk-on part in demonstrations or riots, as required.

Nation states in the Middle East have themselves clearly on a map, but turning from the world described with such insight by Philip Bobbitt, we clearly need a new sheet of paper to draw it.

Chapter 7

Politics

Today's debate about the need for political change in the Middle East is not new, but its scale and political impact are. The Arab world was politically problematic for most of the twentieth century. The new Arab states, created at the Treaty of Versailles which wound up the Ottoman empire, had uncertain starts. By mid-century, the Palestine question had become critical; and, in 1947, the foundation of the state of Israel led to a succession of wars and a sense of grievance that has coloured the outlook of every Arab. The revolutions and coups in the 1950s and 1960s gave the Arab world a reputation for instability, but for regimes during the 1980s and 1990s there was a period of ideological immobility. All this long while, a reinfection of an old Islamist fever was being incubated.

A radical change occurred on 11 September 2001. This is a commonplace, but the depths of how true it is are still emerging. Firstly, the violent overspill of the 'disturbance of spirits' in the Islamic world directly affected the Americans at home, at their enormous distance from the Middle East. This was a moment of hard-edged crystallization, a recognition of how far we had come both in the region and with globalization. It led people to argue that the internal affairs of Arab states, particularly Saudi Arabia, while they might have been private business in the past, were now having direct security implications overseas and therefore were becoming 'our business' too. Hence one voice of the debate about Arab politics was asking, 'What's going on out there? Isn't it time they introduced democracy to relieve some of those tensions? They're generating extremists.'

Secondly, the invasions of Afghanistan and Iraq helped bring into focus for us outsiders a long-running and deep debate inside the

Islamic world about the nature of government – should it be secular or Islamic? What makes government legitimate? Is it simply control of people and territory (a rule of thumb long used by the European powers) and recognition of this by the international community? Or should government have a more internally coherent moral legitimacy which, in the Islamic world, many argue should mean rule in conformity with the *Shari'ah*, the law and prescriptions deriving from the Koran and the traditions of the Prophet?

These two arguments – about the roles of democracy and of religion in government – lie at the heart of the general debate about the Middle East. They contain many latent and unanswered questions and not the least of these are ones about European responsibility for the styles of government instituted after the Treaty of Versailles and what followed them. These questions lie behind the urgent one many in the region now put to us in their anxiety and frustration, 'Do you want stability, or reform – change even at the cost of instability?'

Until January 2006 and the election of Hamas in Palestine, of the 22 members of the Arab League,[1] eight were governed by families and eight by military or revolutionary figures or their immediate successors. Among the remaining six, Iraq obviously used to belong to the military/revolutionary group after overthrowing the Hashimite regime (which was from the first group). The Lebanon, with its unusual demography of sizeable Christian, Sunni and Shi'i elements, was a form of democracy between the end of the French mandate in 1943 and 1975 when a 17-year civil war broke out. It was then dominated by Syria, from the second group. After Syrian 'withdrawal' in 2005 and the assassination of the prime minister, Rafiq al-Hariri, the Lebanese immediately voted in al-Hariri's son who had no previous political experience. It remains an exception to many generalizations about the Arab states. The other four of the

---

1 The members are: Algeria, Bahrain, Comorros Islands, Egypt, Eritrea, Iraq, Jordan, Kuwait, the Lebanon, Libya, Mauretania, Morocco, Oman, Palestine (not yet an independent state, but a full member), Qatar, Saudi Arabia, Somalia, Syria, the Sudan, Tunis, the United Arab Emirates, the Yemen.

remaining six are the Comorros Islands, Somalia, Eritrea and Mauretania.

The last chapter made the case that the 'Abbasids' exercise of power was absolute and a break from the Arabian tradition. Furthermore, owing to the exclusive character of the caliphs' court at Baghdad, the settled population in the north developed a separate culture and way of life in the shadow of the absolute ruler. The Arabian tradition never died out – for a variety of geographical and political reasons: the Ottomans did not have the wherewithal to impose sustained rule on Arabia, apart from the pilgrim road to Mecca. This state of affairs broadly continued to the end of Ottoman rule in the Arab lands in 1918. There was crumble before the Ottoman collapse. In the nineteenth century in North Africa, local governors manoeuvred their way to greater independence and Europeans intervened – in Egypt, Tunis, Algeria and Libya.

The people of today's Arab states thus have a political experience that is fundamentally different from our own. We notice the lack of participation. Whatever may be said about elections in the Arab world and they do, of course, occur, they have not impinged on the rule of the regime. Rulers, whether monarchical, head of family, or revolutionary, have not proved removable at the hands of the people, save by general insurrection. Instead, whatever the operations of elected legislatures, matters affecting the core interests of regimes can be secured through emergency or national security legislation, decrees and the manipulation of appointments. The regime remains the source of power and therefore the key point of reference and influence. Changes at the top can happen, but when they do, they usually do so through the agency of power players within regimes, rather than from outside.

There are constitutions, some of them replacements, but so far they have not had a pre-eminent hold on the rules of politics. The competing aspirations of commitment to a religious code as the supreme model, or the secular counterpart, commitment to a modernizing programme that assumes unquestionable authority, have both had as powerful a voice.

Iraq and Palestine are both sudden and recent exceptions to this generalization. In Iraq, the Americans crushed the regime and insisted on elections. Palestine is not a state and has limited sovereignty. Like Iraq, Palestine has client relationships with outsiders committed to seeing an electoral process. It is not yet possible in either case to see what sort of power centre may emerge. The election of Hamas is a big event and a way point in the region's underlying shift from nationalist to religious politics. Whether the Shi'is in Iraq or the Hamas Islamists in Palestine submit to further electoral chance, remains to be seen. If they do, they will face urgent questions amongst themselves about the implications of pluralism for their own ideologies.

The democratic solution to the problem of power is to make parties compete at regular elections. This presupposes that the parties are free genuinely to compete on clearly distinguishable grounds of ideas and policies. The justification is that this cumbersome and inefficient arrangement expresses a trust in the sense of the people and their commitment to preserve as much of their liberty as possible. Notionally, it puts the people of power at the service of the population whose approbation they need. It should be clear by now that of the four main themes in this book, family, faith, Arab identity and power, the first three are problematic for the development of a party system, or at least of parties which can compete on policies, rather than sectional interests.

Parties built around a religious commitment need, in our terms, a separate look and this comes later. Many Arabs would disagree with this categorization of 'religious' politics and this is an important point to note, if we are to acknowledge their different frontiers of political thought, the relationship they recognize between faith and power. For now, in secular terms, we can say that the idea of political party emerged in the Middle East in the late nineteenth century. It began principally as a close networking of nationalist minded associates brought together by a determination to oppose foreign influence, whether Ottoman or European. *Hizb*, the Arabic term for 'party', had an older history, meaning 'a group of loyal supporters or henchmen' around an individual whose power was autonomous. A rough tribal equivalent would be the *kabir* who leads a *qaum* (a self-selecting group within a tribe) made up of his personal supporters. In a political sense, a leader of this type was supported by his followers, but not dependent on them.

These groupings and parties were small manifestations of power, a determination to put a personality or idea into the public arena. Communism, as an anti-Western, anti-traditionalist credo, offered a bright agenda for renewal and progress. It attracted some intellectuals from an early stage, following the stabilization of the Soviet Union, but it never took a mass hold due to its hostility to religion. On account of Karl Marx's Jewish antecedents, the Saudi monarchy and others were persuaded that communism was simply a Zionist front. Communism only got into power and then just for 30 years as the People's Democratic Republic of South Yemen.[2] In most other Arab countries (even those with good relations with the Soviet Union), being a communist remained an imprisonable offence.

The more significant experience of party life was different. It came of a mutation of the original local idea of party to a different project, a collectivization of popular support for an established group of men of power – either those already in power and looking for a popular legitimization of power, or for those going for power, as the FLN which won the war against the French in Algeria.[3] These parties have little narrative of political competition with other parties like themselves. They have hardly proved to be ecologically cosy organisms.

The *Ba'th*, in Damascus and Baghdad, presents an interesting paradigm of this second type of Arab political party. The party dates itself to 1934 and it came to power in Syria and Iraq in a coup in 1963. Among the co-founders of the movement was a Christian Syrian, Michel Aflaq, who was heavily influenced by his observation of European politics and believed deeply in nationalism and Arab unity. *Ba'th* has no single equivalent in English translation, but has

---

2 A sympathetic account is given by Fred Halliday in his *Arabia Without Sultans* (London, Penguin, 1974).

3 Alastair Horne's *A Savage War of Peace* (London, Macmillan, 1978), gives the best account in English of this struggle. Illustrative of the problem of political categories, the insurgents and the FLN described themselves as 'Muslims'/'Les Musulmans'.

to be suggested with ideas of mission, resurrection and propagation.[4] Strongly secularist among committed party members, the party never adopted outright hostility to Islam, but became rigorous in extirpating Islamist activity which could be interpreted as political opposition. The religious emotion, however, was engaged with the party's standing by an 'eternal message' of socialist reform and justice. The founding members did not last long, but were superseded by stronger personalities competing for supreme power. The new leaders soon changed the dynamic of the party's processes and sense of direction, embracing more socialist ideological positions and, indeed, organizational styles. Doubtless present in their motives was a need to engage the support of the Eastern bloc in the tension with Israel.

In Iraq a branch of the party was opened in 1954 and it also came to power in a coup in 1963. Once in power, the party's vision of itself as a revolutionary vanguard, with many clandestine, almost gnostic, characteristics, inevitably acquired during the years before power, soon precipitated an independent inner circle of leaders and power brokers. Despite further coups at the top, the wider membership found itself consigned to roles of loyalty and collusion, with limited access to promotion and participation at an executive level. In this way, it was easy for the Ba'thist regimes to reinforce their power by the fast building of public sector economies, large military and security apparatuses and civil service structures. Interestingly, this construction of local power centres never caused the party to lay aside its pretension to a supra-national existence and mission. Iraq, in party terminology, was no more than a region for the party's activities; and Syria was another, despite the strong enmity between Damascus and Baghdad, recognizable since the days of the Ummayyads and 'Abbasids. Party membership was indispensable for preferment in a career in any of the state structures. The relentlessness of the leadership, protected by the almost casual elimination

4 The entry in the best Arabic-English dictionary, Hans Wehr's, admits this difficulty by offering 'approximates to Renaissance Party', though Renaissance, an idea popular in modern Arab history, is usually translated as *al-nahdah*.

of opposition or the simply disaffected, institutionalized fear as a factor for discipline and efficiency. Corrupt and lethargic, the party system nonetheless ran well.

A cameo of this experience in Iraq is the story of a bedouin poet who had produced a remarkable ode in praise of Saddam Husain. One night he is unexpectedly telephoned and told a car will collect him immediately. He is taken, with the windows blacked out, on a long journey to a rest house in, he assumes, Baghdad. He is told food will be brought and he is not to leave his room. Never before caged in a building like this, he starts to get seriously depressed. A couple of days later he is woken at 2 a.m. and told to report downstairs. Into another blacked-out car, he is whisked off on a long, circuituous journey, pushed indoors, through some ante-rooms and into the presence of Saddam. He is told to recite his ode which he does, though nervously because it begins with an irony which somebody not very bright could interpret as an insult. All are amazed. Saddam presents him with a plated rifle (which is welcome) and praises him extravagantly. Saddam asks him to make any wish, ask any favour. Overcome by the occasion, he takes incautious courage and mentions the sequestration of some land by the party on which he had wanted to build a house for his son. Saddam dismisses him with a wave of the hand, while declaiming that he will personally cut off the head of anyone who denies the poet his right. Two hours later he is back home. On arrival, he finds the senior local leadership of the party waiting for him. They implore him to accept their revocation of the sequestration and any help he might need in building the house. The haphazard effectiveness of a Middle Eastern bureaucracy is as elemental as a force of nature, once engaged. And it is correspondingly alarming to those who are usually safe in relying on 'system failure'.

It was a commonplace of the Cold War to assume that because the Soviet system lacked integrity, its officials were utterly cynical. So, indeed, many of them may have been, but not all. Power in religion and, no less, in politics imposes the imperative to live with paradox. Many took pride in the achievements of the Soviet system, even if some of the means to the ends were antipathetic. The worker-bee official is deprived of choice by the force of the argument that 'there is no alternative'. Our instinctive desire to dignify our work helps him preserve a residual belief in the possibility of things working out better in the end. And so in Iraq, faced with the regime of the Shah of Iran on one side and the Saudi monarchy on the other, many Iraqi party members would have felt able to explain their commitment to the space left to them as a search for development and on a different course to what they saw as the evils of a Western-supported despot in Iran and the religious neo-puritanism of Saudi Arabia. These feelings would have been only sharpened once al-Khomeini moved in next door in Iran. Finally, and significantly, the world of work is not his defining medium. He belongs, of course, to family more than to power. The job he does is congenial to his education. He is in a position to help others in a wide aspirational sense and, in practice, to lend a hand to family when the need arises. That, after all, is the example he is set from right up the line in the party hierarchy.

The Arab Socialist Union of Nasser's Egypt had less trouble with local opposition, as one would expect in view of Egypt's physiog-nomy and history. Again, its mission was to propagate and deliver the mission, the vision of the leader. At the time, the motives to modernize Egypt and give this powerful culture the status and influence in the region it reckoned its own by right, were urgent and widely shared. After the torpor of the latter days of the Egyptian kingdom and a largely unpopular and involuntary hosting of the Allies during the Second World War, the newspapers and Nasser's powerful rhetoric in long speeches broadcast by 'Voice of the Arabs' gave the population a new sense of pride and much entertainment. Egypt's liberal experiment in the 1920s had not touched the masses. But, like the *Ba'th*, the party was not troubled by competition from another political party (the Muslim Brotherhood was another matter), and the reordering of the party and even its renaming revealed how dependent it was on the immediate political needs of its leadership. Its accessory function was plain to see as was its vulnerability to entropy, only resisted by fear.

Structures engineered and maintained by fear are apparently tolerated, for all their contradiction to the principle of equality between individuals. The intellectual and emotional grip of a strong leader is far more powerful than we usually recognize and to those in the system it is also, to all appearances, welcome. The strong leader absolves responsibility, frames hopes and fears. He reinforces solidarity, so often something which the city dwellers miss. Importantly, he is a bulwark against social chaos which would impinge on the interests of family life, on society at a good remove from the centre of power. He is adept at working the religious anxieties about social conflict, or *fitnah*. The strong leader ruling a republic of nationalist heritage hardly plays the role of the tribal shaikh, but his role can be analogous. He strikes chords which are recognizably part of the same music. The role is personal and not institutional. The shrewdness and cunning of Mu'awiyah are everywhere in evidence.

An element of competition did exist between the parties formed by the Palestinian resistance, known in later days as terrorist groups. Again, ideologues and founders from Christian families were notable. George Habbash and Wadi' Haddad of the Popular Front for the Liberation of Palestine (PFLP) and Nayif Hawatmeh of the Democratic Front for the Liberation of Palestine (DFLP) were Greek Orthodox. They competed, of course, for members and acclaim in their achievements, but not in conventional elections. They relied heavily on Leninist principles of organization, cell structures and committees which gave them high levels of discipline and efficiency in secret operations. Support for their work from the Soviet Union and its satellites, training and funding, reinforced this essentially European style. The Palestinian factions did deal in Palestinian politics. But it is fair to say that their contribution to the life of their community, admittedly scattered in diaspora and exile, or under occupation, was dominated by the attention they gave to the external threat from Israel, or those Arab regimes whom they liked, or disliked. The transition to terrorist activities allowed them to exploit their reputations in levering protection and further funding from nervous Arab politicians whom the factions menaced with threats to their security. The Abu Nidal organization, properly called The Popular Front for the Liberation of Palestine – The Revolutionary Council, was expert at this extortion.

The situation of the Lebanese parties was slightly different. They worked within a constitutional democracy, but also in a country deeply riven by confessional divisions. The Lebanese parties had to submit to elections, but could rely considerably on each sect's natural loyalty to the party which claimed to represent it. Closer inspection reveals a long-standing dominance over the parties by established families and, during the civil war, the war lords who led them. A clannish character is clear and leads us back to the underlying permanence in Arab social life of a collective behaviour that is an extension of the intense gregariousness of the extended family. Family is to the town what tribe is to the desert and countryside.[5]

For this reason, during the years of immobility towards the end of the twentieth century, strong leaders had time to link their interests to their families, even going so far as to open the way for their sons to succeed them. Politics in the Middle East may be, on one level, a reaching out for an idea, Arabism, Arab socialism or renewal, but the focus is personal and the fortunes of parties linked to strong leaders stand or fall according to the fortunes of the leader. The fate of Fatah in the Palestinian elections in 2006 may prove to be a case in point. Yasir Arafat, who personified the movement, died in 2004.

The Arabs' other conventional form of political power today is straightforwardly rooted in the family. There are eight of these regimes. The claims of two originate also in religious prestige. The Hashimites in Jordan were previously the governors of Mecca and they claim descent from the Prophet. The royal family that has ruled Morocco since the end of the eighteenth century similarly claims descent, as *sharifs*, from the house of the Prophet. The other six are the regimes of the member states of the Gulf Cooperation Council (GCC).[6] Three of these regimes are connected by association with the same tribal confederation. The *Al Sa'ud,* in Kuwait the *Al Sabah*

---

5 Hizb Allah, 'The Party of God' in the Lebanon had a different genesis, much influenced by the revolution of al-Khomeini in Iran, and is covered by comments on religious groups in the next chapter.

6 The GCC member states are Oman, the United Arab Emirates, Saudi Arabia, Qatar, Bahrain and Kuwait.

and the *Al Khalifah* in Bahrain are all members of the *'Anaizah* confederation which, paralleled by the (*Qahtani*) *Shammar*, dominates the northern half of Arabia. The extent of the 'conceptual infrastructure' gives these regimes access and influence up into Jordan, Syria and Iraq. The tribes there have blood and cultural links reaching down into the heartland of the Arabian peninsula. The oil wealth visited on these regimes since the 1950s has invigorated these connections.

Unsurprisingly, the experience of independent nationhood gave these countries governed by tribal rulers powerful ideas for underpinning their own security. The main story was doing what was conventional for states to do – have a navy, a ministry of planning and so on. In fact, in very important ways, this cladding of power with an armoury of regulatory, executive and security functions, greatly enhanced the defences of the individuals at the top. In 1966, the Shaikh of Abu Dhabi, Shaikh Shakhbut, was deposed. Though out of power, he was the first ruler of Abu Dhabi to die in his bed for two centuries. His younger brother, Zayid, who succeeded him, ruled for 35 years until his death in 2005. In 1999 when the ruler of Bahrain died, the average length of rule in the GCC member states was 24 years.

The majority of these rulers were formed in a different age. This, due to the cultural attachment to the achievements of the past, is considered greatly to their credit. They knew hardship, learned their lessons at the knees of 'real men', grew up in a simpler world which had time to lay a greater emphasis on what truly matters – values and people.[7] In Arabia, it has been axiomatic until very recent years that a ruler is available to his people.

Modern living has now eroded the accessibility of the rulers. This has also cost the rulers a good argument. They might have been able to say that they were developing an indigenous political formula, using the tradition of consensus which allowed the people due

---

7 A dignified old tribesman in the Empty Quarter said to me 30 years ago, 'We've survived till now by knowing a lot about our camels. Dreadful to think that to survive the next bit our children will have to become mechanics.'

influence on decision-making and a restriction on the use of power by the leader. The *majlis* custom was the practice of the shaikh, or amir, sitting in 'open house' council where any fellow national (or indeed visitor) could turn up and make his petition or view known. This meant accessibility and 'live broadcast' testing for the ruler. His response to those calling on him was plain for all to see and hear. It survived into the 1960s and, exceptionally in some places, until now. The rulers and their ministers were put to the trouble of dealing equitably with the different interest groups and tribes in order to maintain consent. Strongly felt local antipathies to those who might try to 'lord it over' their fellow men, helped keep ruling feet firmly on the ground. The pressures of communications, however, the astonishing wealth from hydrocarbons, always difficult to transfer into the private sector, and the proliferating complexity of the business of state (in particular the need increasingly to deal with others' business as well as their own in the circus of foreign affairs) have almost eliminated these restraints and 'reality checks'.

At family level in the GCC states, the *majlis* system, admittedly for those who can afford the entertainment costs, remains a normal social activity. By turns, formal and awesome, warm and full of noisy laughter (the jester is a social role which someone can be relied on to take up, maintaining a tradition which goes back to the start of tribal life), the *majlis* is the school room of young children and growing men. If Arabs impress us with their social presence, the *majlis* is where they learn it.

The ruling families have not been immune to the bulging demographics of the region and now constitute substantial communities, in effect, set above the level of other citizens and even fellow tribesmen. While not perhaps going as far as the revolutionaries and military rulers in holding tight to themselves the reins of power, the ruling families have become a truly exclusive political class. It is true that they, and their forebears, have been busy coping with the challenges of material development. But for the generations ahead a massive challenge remains of liberating the wealth of their single resource economies. They will find that they need to build political ways of going on which renew the opportunities for wider participation which used, still almost within living memory, to exist.

A discussion of the traditional rulers needs the balance of the human factor and would not be complete without a bow of deference to the quality of these men as remarkable people and personalities. The wide angle view takes in the political trends and challenges, our outsider's concerns about current performance against our own objectives for political security, and does not leave us feeling full of optimism. Encounters with these men, however, do have a powerfully sedative effect. Conscience tugs the sleeve and asks, 'When do we know that people are charming?'[8] But impression management, for all its consummate deftness and knowledge of human nature, is only part of the story. These men have, by comparison with most politicians in the outside world, extraordinary experience of the work which they have to do, and of the people they rule. They share the inherited tribal culture, even if they make large exceptions for themselves. Having to act the parts of a corporate CEO, a politician, a head of state, a judge and a paterfamilias, and yet be for the people something of what they know the people want, is having to play on an emotionally and mentally demanding register. Whether it is the affectionate humour of 'Isa, the late Amir of Bahrain, the dignified courtesy of Khalid, the last but one King of Saudi Arabia, the acumen of Rashid, Shaikh of Dubai, or, in Abu Dhabi, Zayid's strength of character in understanding people, we are only noticing one aspect of extraordinary and complicated personalities. The effect they had on those around them and their ability to shoulder the wants of most of their people for most of the time, were important parts of the state of affairs they left their successors. The rapport and respect occurring between such men and their people is part of the story. It is not necessarily deficient in the other states, but in the traditionally ruled states it is very marked.

The sceptic protests that this apparent irreplaceability is really part of the problem. He says the tendency of power is to reinforce itself and even not to stamp out emerging personality cults. It leaves

8 'When we have been charmed by them.'

no room for the natural competition which might keep sharp the skills of government, and so these skills get behind the game. And that is why the outsiders are raising the volume on the subject of reform. A less sceptical point, already made, bears quick repetition. The Arab world faces some severe problems – the Palestine/Israel problem, prospects for Iraq, Iranian ambitions in the region, proliferation, other new threats of globalization ... and there are others. It is true that a community of nations as homogeneous in outlook as the Arabs, and with so many problems to discuss, will find neighbourhood business a preoccupation. In the cockpit of the Middle East, the pressure of competing foreign interests, during colonial times and through the Cold War, has left the Arabs little time off from receiving visitors. They have developed, as did King Husain in Jordan, an outstanding facility for speaking to a number of audiences at once. It is hard, however, not to feel a concern that foreign affairs, whether in the region or abroad, can start to look like displacement activity. The critical state of foreign affairs admirably disposes of arguments that the time is ripe for reform at home.

Beneath and around these Arab political arrangements, a changing temper is in crescendo. In the current phase, first visible in Egypt and now spreading generally across the region, this is the parallel and independent religious discourse about the right ways to manage the collective life of the community.

The politics of faith, the interface of credo and ego as power centre, are as old as Islam and the debate over the succession to the Prophet. The earliest 'religious' party was possibly the 'party of 'Ali', the *Shi'at 'Ali*, followed closely by those who disagreed with his parleying with Mu'awiyah and whose members in the end killed him, *al-Khawarij*. And so it has gone on. In the last century, tribal partisans of Ibn Sa'ud materially helped enforce his rule across Arabia from his headquarters at Riyadh. They were dubbed '*al-Ikhwan*' ('The Brothers') and they operated as a militarized vanguard for *Wahhabi* teaching, raiding also into Iraq and Jordan. The resonances from the mid-seventh century may be partly misleading, but they vibrate even at our range.

The politics of faith have found controversy in matters of blood and in matters of power – from the succession question of the caliphate to the highly sophisticated mediaeval apologetics about the nature of the 'virtuous city' to the turbulence of today. During the salad days of the 'Abbasids, a line of rationalist thinking made a sophisticated philosophical critique of ethics, taking up the Greek tradition and also developing an independent genre of enquiry. These were the *mu'tazilis* and their influence survived for some hundreds of years from the early ninth century.[9] Thereafter a more conservative and traditionist[10] mood settled on the Islamic world.

The conservative stamp on the one hand, and the flourishing of the Sufi orders (protected by the Ottomans) on the other, meant that dissidents took up ultra-conservative positions. And that has been the score for upwards of six centuries. Those politics were not generally directed at us as outsiders, but at the Muslims themselves. Regimes, in particular, were targets because, it was felt they bore a special responsibility for the apparent weakness of the Islamic community in the face of the encroaching West. And this was exacerbated by the Arab nationalists' yearning to imitate Western nation states. This religious aspect of Arab politics was perhaps, in retrospect, the main theme, but we gave it little attention because it was remote, religious and difficult. We were much more concerned with local attitudes towards ourselves. In short, we have entered the modern era with the empty bag of ignorance over our heads.

9 See George Hourani's *Islamic Rationalism –The Ethics of 'Abd al-Jabbar* (Oxford, Oxford University Press, 1971).
10 This useful technical term applies to those whose arguments were rooted in the tradition and particularly the Traditions (*hadith*) of the Prophet.

Chapter 8

Modernity

In the more lavish Arab offices, familiar gadgets are those big screen clocks which show the time on a glass map of the world on which the passage of daylight is lit up by a patch of brightness which moves from East to West; and the dark areas on either side show which parts of the world are in night. And so it is with modernity: being bright and now, it quickly draws a shadow over what seemed so new so recently. To many young Arabs, the idea that Nasser and other khaki rulers were modern would be laughable. The fact that we in older generations remember these rulers and that they superseded statesmen who wore the fez and whose fathers wore frock coats, is neither here nor there. The whole lot are in history and today they just seem quaint. The Shah of Iran is not a living memory for the majority of the population of the Arab world. Modern is global. We used to think that modern must equal Western. Among the Arabs, this idea is questioned and often rejected.

A proposition with which Arabs under 15 will probably disagree, has the backstop on modernity in 1991. In that year, Saddam Husain's army was expelled from Kuwait. The myth of the khaki classes' invincibility was rudely disturbed by an outside intervention – the sanctuary of non-alignment had gone, along with the Cold War – and the story of Arab unity appeared to be in pause as several Arab armies joined the coalition against Iraq. The invasion of Kuwait had in itself exposed a sharp crevasse beneath the icy surface bonhomie of Arab rulers. In Syria, Jordan and Palestine, a deep but suppressed popular antipathy towards the richer Arabs of the Gulf was exposed. And the northerners, with their revolutionary or Hashimite heritages, were the more pious adherents to the creed of Arab nationalism and unity. The Palestinians – and Palestinian guest workers in Kuwait had been a major proportion of the population before the invasion – had to watch their leadership disastrously decide to show solidarity with Saddam. Some 400,000 Palestinians had to move up to Jordan. Further south and at regime level, association with the United States in the coalition meant collusion with the arrival of non-Muslim troops in Saudi Arabia. Those already hostile to American influence rhetorically expanded their sense of the holy space surrounding the cities of Mecca and Medina to cover the whole country. They declared their outrage and hostility to the Saudi king's decision to call in the Americans. In 2004, the Saudis reached agreement with the US that American bases in Saudi Arabia had to be closed.

During the long crisis over Kuwait, the image of an Arab front against Israel faded and two years later secret negotiations between the Palestinians and the Israelis were revealed which led to the 'Oslo Accords'. Although these accords were not fully implemented, the pan-Arab engagement in the Arab-Israel dispute was noticeably affected. The heady boast of being about to 'burn Israel' which Saddam Husain had used in May 1990 during an Arab summit at Baghdad, had lost its audience. The political obligation on Arab leaders to appear active on the Palestinians' behalf was losing its edge; and the matter was considerably left to the neighbouring states to deal with, as their interests dictated. Egypt, long the dominant influence in the Gaza strip and able to talk with the Israelis on account of their peace treaty, did not back off; the Jordanians, also close to the Americans and mindful of their own large Palestinian population and their traditional influence in the West Bank going back to their inclusion of the West Bank into Jordan between 1948 and 1967, stayed engaged; the Syrians for whom the liberation of the Golan Heights was a matter of upholding the legitimacy of the *Ba'th* regime, made sporadic attempts which later died away, to reach progress in indirect negotiations with the Israelis.

In these years, at regime level, the season was autumnal and personified by the increasingly senior ages of the Arabs' leaders. Secular political thought, so much the theme of the modern era (conventionally conceived as dating from the end of the Ottoman empire) was evanescent. The arrival at the turn of the millennium in Jordan, Bahrain, Syria and Morocco of a new successor generation of rulers lent hope of a rejuvenation of political thought. At the end of the Cold War, the Arab Left was stranded. Regimes which had done well out of playing East-West tensions,[1] found themselves in puzzled baulk.

The underlying political issue (rather below the reach of any regime's ability to influence it) had shifted from Arab identity to religious identity. The region was retuning. The new concern was a discourse about power: who should have it and how should it be exercised. The reference points were not Left or Right, monarchical tradition or the promises of socialism, but fidelity to the example of the early Muslim community.

Khomeini's revolution in Iran, 12 years earlier, had contributed a blow against secularism. It promoted an anti-western sentiment, but it had limited influence on Sunni Islamist thought. To the majority of Arabs who are Sunnis, the Shi'i goings on in Iran were decidedly not their business.[2] They appeared to promote the power of the Shi'i religious establishment in a way which conflicted with the lay and independently minded culture of the Sunni Arabs (and they wanted none of this spreading to their own Shi'i minorities). The Iraqi invasion of Kuwait, however, signalled to the sensitivities of the radicals that Arab governments could not be trusted to prevent tensions breaking out into internecine Arab conflict. Rejection of *fitnah* (conflict in the community) is a religious imperative, as well as a social interest. Its outbreak in the *ummah,* the Muslim community, was an affront, like the arrival of the foreign armies in a Muslim country.

1 An evocative anecdote from 1989 was of the news of the fall and execution of the Romanian communist dictator, Nikolai Ceaucescu, reaching a session of the 'Euro-Arab Dialogue'. The European officials at the table were jubilant ... and then they noticed that their Arab colleagues had remained seated and silent. The face of each was a picture of confusion and apprehension.
2 Khomeini's major book, *al-Hukumah al-Islamiyah* (*Islamic Government*) was written in Arabic, but the first Arab edition did not appear until 1979 in Cairo.

In 1991, a new pulse was felt in the centuries' long story of radical Islam. The Arab *mujahidin*[3] who had successfully fought against the Soviet forces in Afghanistan, were returning home to the Arab lands. Often they only landed to ricochet off into Europe, as Arab regimes tried to round them up on account of the new wave of enthusiasm they were bringing to local dissident and opposition groups. This new breed of Islamists, operational and battle hardened, began to make an impact. From there to the attack on the World Trade Centre in New York in 1993, to the attacks on the US embassies in Nairobi and Dar es-Salaam in 1998, to the attack on the USS *Cole* in the harbour at Aden in 2000, it was a straight run. Again, the problem was not new, but the modern scale of it was. Then the disaster of 9/11 made outsiders realize that terrorists could strike on a strategic level and deep inside our own defences. The mental associations of 'The Middle East' no longer connected with Israel and 'The Middle East Dispute'. The threat of terrorism was now the chief concern. This required a wider vision and the hitherto quiet and private life of Arabia had to be included in the view. For Arabs from Arabia, along with some Egyptians and others, were significantly implicated in the terrorist events.

At the level of regimes, there was a noticeable fall off in collective Arab political action. At the popular and street level, another trend was working the other way. The North African states and Sudan might appear caught up with their own business and local interests, but extreme Islamist nationals from all these countries were gravitating towards the emerging purpose of a transnational, meta-secular endeavour – *Jihad*. Rejectionists and oppositionists in the radical religious trend had traditionally been caught up in the political issues of their own countries, even though many of these were seen to arise from foreign influence. Not even the Muslim

---

3 This word comes from the same linguistic root as *jihad*. A *mujahid* is one who is engaged in *jihad* – a good example of contemporary controversy: in the past translated as 'holy war' (cf. the campaigns to spread Islam and campaigns against the Byzantines), it is now played down by some; those in Afghanistan meant by it 'fighting the Russians' who at the time were atheists and were invading the *Dar al-Islam*.

Brotherhood, the oldest contemporary organization of radical Islamists, had managed to maintain a wide and coherent international
agenda, try as they might on the subject of Israel.

The new verve for internationalist cooperation among the most
committed activists gave these movements and groupings an
unexpected lease of life. The networks stretched from the Sudan to
Scandinavia, from Mauretania to Mazari-Sharif, to say nothing of
gathering strands of connection across Africa into the Islamic
societies of the Far East, Central Asia and the former Soviet Union.
The Islamists' detailed political conflicts with local regimes were
occluded by a new emphasis on resisting the Westerners, and the
Americans in particular, inside the *Dar al-Islam.* That is how it
seemed to us, but our own knowledge of this hitherto obscure
dimension of local politics had been minimal. We had probably
underestimated the true depth and scale of the Islamist influence in
Arab societies. There were few with the expertise and language skills
to observe it and it had seemed so local. What struck us was the new
and sharp focus on the West.

I was posted to our embassy in Cairo in 1978 and remember my
first meeting with Richard Mitchell who was visiting there when I
arrived. He had written the classic work on the Muslim Brotherhood,[4] based on his PhD fieldwork in Cairo in the early 1950s when
the Brotherhood was at its most powerful. As I approached Richard
at his café table, he was trying to greet me and at the same time
angrily wave his newspaper at me. He had that morning received
news that the Ford Foundation would not fund a research project he
wanted to lead on Islamism. As he showed me, every article on the
front page of his *Herald Tribune* was relevant to his subject or its
context. It would be a decade before the generation of Westerners
interested in the Middle East and brought up on a diet of Arab
nationalism would really recognize Islamism as a deep problem,
deep rooted and capable of deep growth.

The intellectual argument behind the growing emphasis on direct
confrontation with the West was that the Americans stood behind

---

4 *The Society of the Muslim Brothers* (Oxford, Oxford University Press, 1969).

the so-called corrupt regimes of the region, seen as so unresponsive to the call to a purer Islam. So the Americans had to be taught that the Middle East would no longer be a comfort zone. American support for regimes would be at a high cost. Hitting Westerners' economic interests and symbols of their materialism came onto the Islamist agenda, a more absolute assertion that the Muslims had in their own hands the defence of their realm and, indeed, the possibility of renewing the face of the earth.

Through the 1990s regime response was mechanical and involuntary. Faced with serious security problems, they set about the Islamist movements and extremists with a white-knuckled determination. As an unintended consequence, the already wide networks of Islamists operating across the Arab diaspora in Europe and elsewhere were enlivened by the new arrivals, activists from Afghanistan, Pakistan and Arab Islamic groups. These were on the run from regimes which were clamping down hard. They sought refuge in havens abroad, in the clandestine capillaries of globalized societies in the West. There they met up with second-generation children of immigrants and infused a new passion of dissent. This played on the sensitivities of anonymity and displacement to which many of the young in minority communities were vulnerable. Liberal Western governments faced sharp criticism from Middle Eastern regimes for harbouring the fugitives.

In the early years of the twenty-first century, an ironic riddle, dimly perceived before by a few specialists, has been making itself felt. Arabs who, with strongly traditional social backgrounds and customs, did not seem particularly equipped to surf the rollers of the modern world, turned out to be extraordinarily adept and evolutionarily agile in exploiting the new possibilities of instant communication and easy travel. For much of the twentieth century, we had regarded tribal people as marginal, attractive to a suspect few for their nostalgia value in evoking the days of T. E. Lawrence and the Arab Revolt, but uninteresting, if not irrelevant, in the contemporary and Westernized sophistication of international affairs. Then, to our surprise, individuals whose remote ancestors had cooperated across the sudden expansion of Islamic empire, Yemenis with Iraqis, Nejdis with Syrians, turned out in today's world to be able to make the tribal conceptual infrastructure merge and connect intercontinentally with the outreach of new technology. In 2001, they had played a big role in 9/11. From 2003, they were shooting at the victorious coalition forces in Iraq and to some effect. They had, it appeared suddenly, got to centre stage, not themselves up in lights, but interfering with the main action and acquiring the prestige, in the circles of international security buffs, of being included among 'New Threats'.

Interestingly, they appeared to be able to cooperate operationally with those from outside their own immediate culture: Egyptians, Sudanese or Algerians were among them. Or seen the other way about, individual Egyptians, Sudanese and Algerians, from countries so long the spear carriers for a new regional secular renaissance, turned out to be able to work the Arab system of social interaction, sponsorship and guarantee, and with new friends from deep in Arabia. More surprising still, apparent alliances sprang up and leapt the barriers of Arab identity, creating operational bonds with Chechens, Europeans, Africans, Pakistanis and operators from further east. Islam, in another version from the one befriended by regimes, was pushing for a new power.

The ugly headline of a terrorist event is violence and the injustice done to the victims and their community. Like the augury most feared by the ancient Greeks, a terrorist act strikes as lightning from a clear sky. Beforehand, a mind bent on violence is in our midst, but invisible to us. The individual ready to commit violence is anonymous to us and therefore beyond dialogue. Without his name, we cannot speak to him and a broader search for dialogue is snagged psychologically by sharply differing points of departure. Attitudes to death and violence in the Middle East are quite simply different to our own. There, the violence of warfare, civil strife, physical abuse by family members or law-enforcers, and judicial penalties are home truths which are in the common stream of experience. Revulsion felt by individuals – by no means rare – at continuing capital punishment is affected by sensitivity about the plain religious prescription of the death penalty in certain cases.

This is hard enough for us to reach, but the mindset which determines that suicide is legitimate when inflicting violence on the other, defies our understanding. Conversations with Arab friends about the motives of the suicide bomber centre on ascribed feelings of frustration, anger and despair, honour and faith. This means something but does not adequately explain what is happening. The religious argument in favour of terrorist suicide holds little ground at the individual level – few concur with it, but socially, collectively, it clearly has some explanatory attraction. The fact is that the families of those who commit suicide, can find themselves, as they receive people who come to offer condolences, being congratulated on the achievement of the deceased. We cannot judge if this is an authentic expression of conviction. What is clear is that suicide, though very rare and considered dishonourable in the Arab world as a personal act, does not, as a political act, necessarily impeach honour. This says something about a comprehensive enmity towards the world of the victims and everything to do with it. This absolute enmity obscures the thing it claims, justice.

Our own Western attitudes come from a different direction. We simply do not accept any analogy with our own use of widespread bombing in 'formal' or 'conventional' warfare. Over there, the argument remains open. Many notice the Western refusal to offer statistics for civilian losses during the wars against Iraq. It is not a matter of relativism, but of *lex talionis*, blood calling out for blood. Honour, blood, a conviction of absolute rightness and a self-abnegating quest for justice, all hover somewhere in the mystery of the suicide's motives. The sociological analyses of deprivation as a factor may be there too in the background, but they are hard to weigh, especially for generalizations. The truly alarming point is that there appears to be no shortage of candidates for suicide missions. And, as we have seen in Israel and Palestine, the candidates are not impassioned to self-destruction, but ready to wait, and wait a long while, during ceasefires and truces, for their orders to go ahead with their self-destruction. The whole matter of timing, why the suicide attacker launches on a particular day, still awaits adequate research. Sectarian extremists of this kind have something in common with members of millenarian movements. A fascinating assertion in Steve Rayner's research on a completely different style of communist enclavists[5] is that millenarian beliefs can only be maintained in a social environment in which it is possible to foreshorten time and compress geographical space. One thinks then of the Islamists' vivid conviction about the appropriateness today of the Islamic community's way of life at the time of the Prophet, the deep outreach in a globalized world and the conviction that the present epoch is finite and known to be ending shortly. There are hints here towards understanding the apparent haphazardness of some attacks, or at least a reminder that we are confronting a mindset not simply disturbed by deprivation, but oriented on the bearings of a compass we do not share.

A problem that we do share with non-extremists and the Arabs generally is the difficulty of defining the borderlands between Islamist commitment and extremism, between extremism and involvement in active terrorism. Legally, here in our own world, these are critical distinctions, but there the conversation is moody, depending on the closeness to home of the threat. One can hear different attitudes to opposition to coalition forces in Iraq and to bombings at home. It is sobering to hear reduced concern when the casualties are foreigners, Shi'is or Kurds.

Islamists command respect in their own communities, even if it is grudging. They are showing fidelity in a society where God is more real than demonstrable facts. They position themselves against a background of carefully selected scriptural arguments and broad imperatives; the less observant around them find themselves located against a background of political expedient and implications of collusion with the non-Muslim world. Absolutist confronts equivocator; the strategic stands against the tactical. Appeals to the authority of religion open no new promising common ground. It is a deaf difference of attitude. The outsider generalizations about

5 Rayner, Steve, 'The Perception of Time and Space in Egalitarian Sects: A Millenarian Cosmology' in *Essays in the Sociology of Perception* (London, Routledge and Kegan Paul, 1982).

Muslims are keenly felt. They strike hard and the subliminal assumptions of which they are well aware, that there is a grey area between the radical Islamists and the extremists is acknowledged. If, save in a forensic sense, we find the distinctions difficult, so do they.

The growing influence of the Islamists, a perceived bias towards stricter observance projected by a minority in the community, is a sensitive but common topic of conversation. People recognize that the Islamists are well organized and effective. Their project may be strategic and often ill-defined, but they know very well how to handle tactical detail, in politics, the law and education. Outside security circles that have to take a more operational stand against extremists, it is hard not to notice a general sense of impotence, a simple inability to know how best to counter the Islamist trend. When Islamists' commitment is seen to move across the border into politics (a border defined by our terms, not theirs), the local individual reaction is often a deep detachment.

Religious activity has traditionally stood astride the two main camps in society, regime and people. The military, the third camp, has always preserved the language of religion – martyr is the word for someone killed in action. Civic society, principally through the sophisticated *waqf* system,[6] funded many educational and welfare needs of the community, as well as mosques. Yet regimes also needed religious officials and courts; and the responsibilities of the state *muftis*[7] gave them purchase on the *'ulama* of their times. Thus, to ordinary people, the Islamist seems to pose a deep-reaching challenge about the life of the community and, at the same time, to be an official problem which only the regime is in a position to address. Detachment is of course endemic about the interests of governments and the muddles governments get themselves into. And this may explain the docility of the so-called 'Arab Street'. The 'Arab Street' is often mentioned by commentators and journalists as a volcanic threat to stability when great issues are at stake, like the

6 A *waqf* – plural *awqaf* – is a trust or benefaction for religious or philanthropic purposes.
7 A *mufti* issues *fatwahs* – canonical statements of advice which are accepted as morally or legally binding.

prospect of coalition action against Iraq. But then, in modern times, this threat does not emerge. It is not that it never does – riots were common in the 1950s and 1960s, but we cannot depend on it. A reason may be the ready awareness of the near impossibility of the individual being able to do anything about such macro events. This nudges people further into a sense of detachment. The Arab's powerful sense of the absurd tends to stave off the depression of these painful realizations with stoic humour and this, of course, only goes down well in a domestic setting. We do not have to look far in the story of our own past century in Europe to see populations of apparently sensible and cultured people being badgered by pressure groups into unexpected and ultimately disastrous and horrifying positions.

The modern Arab has much to contend with in the home scene before lifting his gaze to a further horizon and considering the generally poor reputation the last 15 years have given his part of the world. Before that, the problem of Israel had kept the nerve strings taut for decades and created a sense of frustration and powerlessness among the people. They were exhorted to high expectations by official rhetoric, and yet could only be spectators of the militarily disastrous record which even Sadat's 1973 Ramadan war did not really erase. The damage done by this problem to education, culture, self-worth and self-knowledge can only be wondered at. It has been a powerful factor in generating the 'victim mentality' which perspicacious Arabs admit has burdened recent generations.

Those who grew up in this period since 1991 may have taken as normal the powerful forces of globalization which engaged during the 1990s with the communications revolution of the Internet, mobile phones and satellite broadcasting. Those who were a little older, have mostly swum in the new currents with surprising ease. The 'conceptual infrastructure' of tribal Arabia was massively empowered. The gregariousness of the Arab, the natural aptitude for networking and capacity to deal across deep horizons were given new strength and outreach. The microcosm of globalization already to be found in the community of the Arab world was illuminated by technological possibilities. International travel became easier and cheaper and its perils of separation were reduced by the mobile phone. The Arab world, despite its dismal scores by international standards for access to computer technology,[8] found itself connected up and linked more closely with its diaspora. Governments and regimes entered a period of caution and stiffness, but ordinary people found new ranges open to them on the airwaves and highways of the Internet. And on these new connections, the terrorists found they could insert themselves into the general hubbub with a clandestinity which defied the conventional defences of a liberal world itself caught up with the energizing possibilities of its own discoveries and innovation.

Characteristic of this new era was the setting up by the Qataris of *al-Jazirah*, the satellite television station which employed Arabs from across the region and broadcast, so long as they were not rude about the Qatari shaikhs themselves, whatever they wanted to say. This Hyde Park corner atmosphere put a ghastly cold light on the efforts of others' TV stations. The two Saudi channels liberally programmed with Koran reading, sports and wildlife documentaries were known as *Ghasab 1* and *Ghasab 2* (roughly, 'Coercion 1' and 'Coercion 2'). Across the region, the flat-roofed and slab-sided shapes of Arab cities sprouted a profusion of satellite dishes. In the northern desert, on a hawk-trapping expedition in 1993, I watched Iraqi satellite television off a dish which my companions had had made from a *saj*, the wok-shaped utensil on which the bedouin make *shrak*, their air-mail version of flat bread.

Al-Jazirah broke the armlock of governments on the Arab media. The BBC and to a lesser extent Radio Monte Carlo had been the old and conventional sources of authority for news and comment, foreign but favoured for their apparent independence of local regimes. Now, as a BBC TV service in Arabic was bought by Saudis and suppressed, the Arabs had their own station which, for its readiness to broadcast what would certainly not be allowed by

8 According to the UNDP's Arab Human Development Report (2003), the Arab world has the lowest scores of the seven world regions, with registered Internet users estimated at about 7 per cent of the population – lower than sub-Saharan Africa.

government-controlled stations, appeared to have its own authority. More interestingly, complex and not very articulate views were debated in chat shows and phone-ins and given a new currency and therefore popular standing. Dislike of Saddam's rule, but rejection of the US-led operation which threw him out in 2003, distrust of terrorism but fascination with Usamah bin Ladin's actions against the West (and Saudi Arabia) were cases in point. Programmes for women and for children placed their interests and welfare in the public space in a new way, leading to changes in newspapers and magazines and also in national media.[9]

Globalization offers the individual an eagle's overview of the world and the eagle's ability suddenly to focus on detail. The Google effect is energizing. The individual's sense of choice is enhanced and so is the inclination to observe and judge. In 1972, I was asked for a view in a late-night argument in a tent as to whether London and Washington were both in England (an interesting question, if taken literally). Arguments today about the way of the world are packed tight with facts and, noticeably, percentages. The bulging demo-graphic problems of the Arab world create serious employment problems for the young. Those who are having difficulty in finding work now speak in terms of the macro problem and its statistics, not only at home but regionally, to voice their frustration.[10] A paradigm shift in the discourse about many subjects which are the ingredients for a political agenda is under way. Religion, which is posing the penetrating questions about the nature of government, remains the hard topic.

Wilfred Thesiger was so influenced by his experience of life among the Arabs of the desert that he took pride in his lack of

---

9 Interesting analyses of the story of Arab satellite TV is contained in Naomi Sakr's *Satellite Realms* (London, IB Tauris, 2001) and Hugh Miles's '*al-Jazeerah – How Arab TV News Challenged the World* (London, Abacus, 2005).

10 Population statistics in the Middle East are hazardous. Hourani (see *op. cit.*) offers the following historical estimates for Cairo: beginning of fourteenth century – 250,00; end seventeenth century – 300,000; 1917 – 800,000; 1937 – 1.3 mn; 1960 – 3.3 mn; mid-70s – 6.4 mn (see his *op. cit.*). In 2002, the Greater Cairo metropolis was estimated to have a population of 14.8 mn.

possessions. He used to say that everything which he valued (save, of course, his collection of books) would fit into a saddle-bag. He wanted to travel light through life and he did so, even though he retained his deep attachment to the traditional. In fact, despite carefully managed appearances to the contrary, he had an understanding view of the Arabs' easy accommodation with what the modern world has offered them. What astonished Wilfred was the speed at which the modern world had overrun them. He was no longer alive on 1 September 2004 when three people lost their lives in the crush to gain access at the opening of a new IKEA shop in Jedda. He would not have been surprised. As far as possessions go, the modern Arab has no difficulty at all in embracing the new. An elderly tribal shaikh who visited me in London and who shared Wilfred's outlook, vituperated against the mobile phone as a thoroughly vulgar habit now sweeping across the younger generation. He had just seen a young Arab in a London street holding a mobile to each ear. For the shaikh this was *degringolade* for the tradition of Arab manners. Not so for the young. The 'push button' generation is globalized and the young Arab takes his place in it as of right. His sense of tradition is not attached to the material world. The National Trust culture of conservation and an emotional involvement with the artefacts of the past are not his. I took a bedouin friend round my favourite places in Rome. He was appalled, 'Mark, this is frightful ... as bad as Damascus – all so old.' Another with whom I visited a small market town in the Cotswolds, asked me why the English liked to live in a museum.

In a book I wrote about falconry in Arabia in 1978, I grappled with the Arabs' facility with what is new and commented that to own a Mercedes is not to enter the society which made it. The intervening years seem to have underlined the point. The technology of the outside world is seen as low-lying fruit which may be picked without endeavour and which, for those who pick, introduce no moral dilemma or consequence. The fascinations with arms purchases, with hi-tech communications equipment, GPS and the latest design of car seem natural and, for a fortunate minority in the oil-producing states, the money to acquire them is on hand, in the bank.

The purchase of labour-saving and comfort gadgets is only common sense, as the woman making yoghurt in the washing machine pointed out. Shopping in the Gulf today, especially in Dubai, one can find new models and upgrades which have yet to be released to the European market. The Arabs will road-test any new item as soon as it appears, and exhaustively. As consumers, they live in comfortable symbiosis with the producers of consumer goods in the Far East.

The materialism, if that is what it is, of a lifestyle which imposes a need for more possessions, draws yet more lines of emphasis under the individuality of the modern person. The gradients for the young are steep – housing, the cash costs of city life, to say nothing of starting a new family – and they are well aware that their needs are ultimately individual rather than collective, no matter how much they may still think in terms of the wider family. The continuing urbanization and greater difficulty of collective living in the cities and towns makes matters worse. The new incomers feel dislocation not only from relationships, but values too. Identity goes under the plough of change as it turns over conventional notions.

For, subliminally of course, on this tide of newness, other items apart from the latest goods and gadgets are also washed ashore – ideas and assumptions. The idea of the modern contains challenges. If they were not readily recognized at first, their implications are now working, and working fast, through the societies of the Arab world.

The situation of the shaikhs is instructive. The shaikhs of tribes are still expected to be sources not only of advice, judgement in conflict, intervention with outsiders (like government) and sponsorship, but also of hospitality and welfare. The costs of this role are climbing steeply and have been for a long time, not only in providing for people in hand-outs and reputation-maintaining acts of generosity, but also representationally in cutting the kind of profile that will secure the attention of regimes and government offices. One solution is to look after oneself first, save massively on the cost of visitors and accept a marginalization from the life of the tribe which supplies, ultimately, the honour of name and function.

Another is to get close to one of the very rich regimes and, in return for a low profile, collect a considerable stipend. This probably means that, when faced with demands to reach further into the pocket than can be afforded, and which would require disturbing the silent contract with the authorities, the shaikh has just to shrug his shoulders and complain at the way of the world. Few there are who can run profitable businesses and remain available to those who need them, and fewer still who can live in relative poverty and yet retain their prestige for fixing, resolving and representing, through force of personality and moral stature. The impression made by such men, even on brief encounter, is unforgettable. Consequently, the shaikhs are fraught and, of course, at the mercy of their own immediate families who require education and the material accessories that the younger generations believe are necessary to their credibility.

A sad consequence in poorer settled tribal communities is the slow disappearance of the *majlis*, open house system, especially at meal times. People live behind walls now, not in tents which, with one side open during the day, encourage callers. So people are less easily summoned, or called by the noise of the coffee being ground (this used to be an open invitation to join in the receiving of a visitor). Poorer people are shy of arriving at a door in a wall at a meal time. They also know that they can never ever repay hospitality which now has to be arranged on more formal terms. Those who used considerably to live off others' meals – a generosity happily given in a close-knit community – now go without. Quite unexpectedly, with children working away from home, malnutrition and attendant health problems are creeping back in.

The Arab response to the modern has been uneven. A superb confidence and dexterity, particularly among the young, walk hand in hand with an outlook which tells us that change is not welcome – either to the Islamists or the regimes who for their own reasons resent the closer integrations of globalization. For both, the outcomes of external interference can appear apocalyptic. The one sees the opportunities for a dramatic new conflict; the other sees the threat of outsiders changing the rules of the game. Amid the novel excitements, the young and the vulnerable see new individual pressures and macro-economic uncertainties. For everyone, the experience of Iraq, its urgent past and opaque future, makes a parable of our own times.

Chapter 9

Language and Signals

The main characteristic we notice on first encounter with the Arab world and which can fill a lifetime with interest, is the language, Arabic. We have already seen its importance as the medium of identity in pre-Islamic Arabia; as the 'language which God spoke' in revelation; as the armour put on by the early 'Abbasid caliphs to defend their Arab rule; as the language of the tradition of Islamic learning and piety; and as the unifying dimension of a new cultural and political trend which sought freedom from the Turks in the nineteenth century, Arab nationalism.

Arabic to the Western ear sounds quite harsh and emphatic. It has guttural consonants not found in Indo-European languages and only three vowels (a, i and u). The cursive alphabet, easily mistaken on the page for a line of barbed wire, is not difficult to learn, but for us the common experience is that it takes a long while before the mind does not freeze when first picking up a page of print. In the early days, the fact that short vowels are not usually written in, despite their importance for the meaning, makes deciphering a text quite a toil. One feels that one cannot get at the meaning unless one already knows what is being meant in the first place.

As a good general rule for outsiders, Arabic is not a language which can be 'picked up'. It is no discouragement but only a home truth to say that a course of introductory lessons usually only leads to a fading of enthusiasm and a loosening grip on the little already learned. Language schools make easy money from this and from the efforts of the stubborn to have another go. The courses hardly ever need to offer anything advanced. Young British diplomats who are supposed to be fairly bright take one-and-a-half years of full-time study to get to a limited standard of interpretership. They used to have to learn 25 new words a day, month in month out, to be sure of a workable vocabulary. My tutor at Oxford told me in a moment of despair that I should not lose hope, the first 25 years were the worst. He was not wrong.

The Arabs often speak of their language as a sea. It is a sea which contains fantastic colours against the light, curious currents, not a few storms and, on the finest days, unreachable horizons. Yet, more than many other languages, Arabic generously repays effort. Arabs are delighted by anyone who tries their language. They, after all, find it hard too. For the majority of Arab school-children, the Arabic Language papers are the toughest subject in their end of secondary school exams. Sacred studies developed a painstaking analysis of every linguistic feature of the text of the Koran. This led to a sophisticated formal grammar of the language. Few are the Arabs who master this. Yet, I have not met an Arab who could not be moved by a demonstration of such mastery. Intimate and demanding, his contact with his God and key to a civilization of religious thought, the language exerts a powerful hold on the Arabs' emotions. The word for Arabic in their own language is feminine. And one of the Arabs' own proverbs springs to mind, 'Three things there are that no man can know: the place of his death, where it will rain, and what is in the mind of woman.' Realizing that for most Arabs their own language contains a good measure of mystery is an important guide in exploring the personality of the way they are.

The high register of classical Arabic, the literary language of the early mediaeval centuries, stands on the shoulders of the pre-Islamic tribal oral tradition of poetry and narrative and of the religious texts. The poet has always had a special place in Arab society. The poet not only has a rare affinity with the language, but a gift for announcing and preserving fundamental truths about the Arab's condition. He articulates the story of the tribe, hands on its values and reaffirms its identity. Competitions for poets reciting their own works at festivals and public events date from deep in the pre-Islamic past until today with special TV programmes and newspaper coverage. Though I know of no research to examine and confirm this, the common view I have encountered is that poets are born and not taught. The capacity to create odes with brilliant linguistic devices, rhymes, images and messages is a matter of genius and no one can explain how this arises. Poets themselves simply shrug and smile that 'it happens'. The gift just manifests itself and its recipient, if he collaborates with it and gives poetry to the people, gains a recognition which sometimes seems to be a recognition of the preternatural. The poet also connects his listeners with the highlands of pride which stand in the remote past of the Arabs' classical age.

The efforts launched by the 'Abbasids to record the 'pure Arabic' of the tribes (see p. 82 above) must have faced many difficulties. There is a book to be written looking at the accuracy of some of the meanings and usages collected by those venerable Baghdadi scholars. Their own understanding of the desert scene was to a good extent that of the voyeur. Money and other inducements were handed out to bedouin who supplied from memory poetic texts and other linguistic bric-a-brac. They would have competed for access to the sources of this easy money. They would have enjoyed themselves and, as must have happened on occasion, amused their powerful sense of humour by retailing obscure and deniable disinformation.[1] What is interesting is that the scholars' findings quickly set like concrete into a monumental tradition the authority of which was not to be questioned.

This quest for cultural authenticity said much about what was happening at that time to the Arabs at Baghdad, but the quest's impact was radical and long term. The text dictated to the Prophet by the archangel Gabriel as the Koran was the exemplar of Arabic and we have already seen how a literalism in understanding this text

1 A modern example of this can be found in *Portrait of a Desert* (London, Collins, 1966) by a team of ornithologists who surveyed the Jordanian oasis at Azraq. They record information from a tribesman that grease from a Saker falcon is good for old skin and that the houbara bustard was hardly ever found in the district. When I raised this with the shaikh of the main tribe around Azraq, ten years later, there was an uproar of laughter that the tricky bedouin had scored a hit on the prurient foreigners – trapped Sakers at that time sold for thousands of pounds, not for boiling up but as the Arab falconer's premier bird – and the houbara is its favoured quarry. No bedouin would say where valuable quarry is to be found. If he knew, he would be off to catch it.

has survived until our own times. But, additionally, the canons of Arabic for ordinary and literary use were framed by this nostalgic quest for the real 'language of the Arabs'.

In 1291, five centuries after the death of the grammarian Siba-waih's (see p. 83), Jamal al-Din ibn Mukarram ibn Manzur finished his great dictionary, *The Tongue of the Arabs*. It remains a major authority in its field. A recent edition[2] runs to 18 volumes. Yasin al-Ayubi's[3] analysis of the quotations used by Ibn Manzur to explain Arabic meanings, shows the following remarkable results: Koranic verses 12 per cent, Traditions of the Prophet 15 per cent, various prose texts 20 per cent and poetry 53 per cent. The poetry quotations by era are made up as follows: pre-Islamic poets 40 per cent, poets whose lives spanned the coming of Islam 10 per cent, poets writing at the time of the first four caliphs 15 per cent, Umayyad poets 30 per cent and 'Abbasid poets 5 per cent. Thus for those who were not still desert dwellers, Arabic became, like family silver, the older the better and a treasured inheritance which affirmed the present. But as with hallmarks, the meanings, origins and age of this inherited Arabic needed skill and attention to understand. We appreciate something of the cultural depth and significance of Arabic when we consider that less than 5 per cent of examples given in this major dictionary are dated later then the year 750. The religious texts have an authority of their own, but Arab sensibility also reveres, despite its pagan culture, the language of pre-Islamic Arabia.

The new Arab states had this inheritance from which to make their everyday language in common. This is what is sometimes called 'standard Arabic' – Arabic which meets most of the requirements of classical grammar, but which is easier and has a much smaller vocabulary. This is the language of public address, of the press, of news broadcasters and airline cabin crew, comprehensible, but standing little comparison with its ancestral models. This is skimmed milk and not cream. Of course, this is a language for daily practical use ('Passengers will find their life jackets under somebody

---

2 *Lisan al-'Arab li-ibn Manzur* (Beirut, 2000).
3 See his *Mu'jam al-Shu'ara fi Lisan al-'Arab* (Beirut, 1980).

else's seat') and not treasure chosen by successive generations from the deposit of faith and literature.

In the 'real world', away from the regime media and the tannoy, the everyday tongue is an Arabic which does retain vitality and the colour of region and history. Spoken Arabic has a wide variety of dialectical forms and outside influences. Close to home, Arabs can identify each other's origins by their accents and language. They can leave each other in the dark by diving deeper into local usage. Further afield they may have difficulty in properly understanding each other. Vocabulary varies enormously, particularly for everyday items like bread, and there are many 'false friends' for the unwary or over-confident outsider, easy but embarrassing errors. Spoken Arabic is not written down (save in cartoon speech bubbles) because it does not conform to the classical or standard rules. As Niloofar Haeri points out in her brilliant study of Egyptian colloquial,[4] spoken Arabic is the mother tongue of the Arabs; classical Arabic is not. The psychological, educational and even political implications of this fact have been visible throughout Arab history as elites of power and religion, the closeness of family and tribal community, and the appeal of Arabism have plaited the strong ropes of continuity and constraint which hold the Arab world together. Spoken Arabic has very strong personality, but those ropes of continuity and constraint are mutating: cables of globalization are bypassing the regional. So local accents and variants are under some threat; the oral tradition of poetry is at risk; and the determination to enter the ranks of the educated who can use spoken 'standard Arabic' nudges people away from the voice they use at home.

Good Arabic is precise. Once in the silk *suq* at Damascus, the owner of an alcove-like shop noticed me looking around his things from the passageway. 'Anything in particular?' I said something about bits of silk for my inkpot. 'Ah, you want *liqah*.' This is the neat disyllable for the raw silk threads which an Arab calligrapher puts into an inkpot to ensure that when he dips in his reed pen, the pen only collects just enough ink and does not put a large blot onto the

4 *Sacred Language, Ordinary People* (New York, Palgrave Macmillan, 2003).

paper. I knew the word from my calligraphy lessons. It had not occurred to me to use it in the market. How wrong I was. I bought enough to last my lifetime. Each of the 150-odd words for the lion captures some special feature or association of the animal. But this precision depends on cultural bias. Mediaeval Arabs had a practical interest in lions which were by no means uncommon in the deserts and along the rivers. The great mediaeval essayist, al-Hariri, writes of '*the* lion' when it appears in his stories because it was simply the lion the traveller was dreading to meet anyway. But Arabic is short of words for flowers because gardening, for the obvious reason that water is scarce, has not been a popular interest. Sir Geoffrey Arthur, a distinguished Arabist who used to read the whole Koran every year, told me he once put a passage of Aristotle alongside its translations in Latin, English, French, German and classical Arabic. The Arabic version came close after the Latin for economy and elegance of translation.

Just as the 'Abbasids wanted to cleave to the Arabic of legitimacy, so today's regimes also reach out for the dignity of elevated standard Arabic. This is impression management on the air and, sometimes, it can be impressive. More impressive, to my own mentality, was President Sadat in Egypt who used to start with a few lines of high and rhetorical diction, sounding like any other ruler, and then in impatience, because he was not very good at it and wanted to press on, he would break down into broad Egyptian colloquial. The Egyptians were, in turns, appalled at his uncouthness (Sadat used to boast he had not been to university, but had spent three years in a British prison – 'just as good') and, in turns, they loved it. Once the president was into a comfortable colloquial canter, they could enthuse with his sharp anecdotes about other Arab leaders and relate to his appeals to homely values and the prejudices of the market-place. He was good at this. It was a political master class. In a secular setting, the self-conscious, portentous ascent on a carefully prepared text (checked, of course, by a court specialist) can lack immediacy and even sincerity. In a religious setting, the faithful will listen to long sermons with attention and deep emotional engagement, enjoying and being uplifted by an oratory they could not begin to imitate. The Islamist trend, of course, prides itself on its standard, if not classical, Arabic. But their tendency to sound bossy means their tone can be divisive and anything but encouraging to the listener. I used to note that al-Shaikh al-Sha'rawi, a famous TV and radio preacher in Egypt knew exactly how to close with his audience by careful use of the colloquial. He may have been charitably providing the president with cover, but his psychology, as he suggested a less strident version of Islam, was as shrewd.

Using Arabic as an impression management trick is returned by the common man in contact with officialdom and power. The supplicant's tone of the petition is, to our tastes, baroque in its beseeching. It took me a long time to realize how seriously meant is this observance of formality. I had assumed this was an easy conventionality, if not irony. Again, I was quite wrong. There is a need for a demonstration of respect for protocol and the rigours of rank which is perceived to give pleasure. This was one of the features of Arab life which brought home to me the great distance which lies between people and power. The linguistic impression management sees to it that the distance is not just observed, but maintained. It is a matter of ingratiating the other and, at the same time, defending one's own. Until the mid-twentieth century, such customs were more common in the north, the Levant and North Africa, in the Ottoman world; in Arabia proper, they were foreign. Arabs could address their kings, princes and shaikhs by their first names and that was that. No disrespect was meant or taken. The natural flair for courtesy in so gregarious a people needed no hyberbole. In other parts, I have sometimes asked about the formality of speech between officials who work, live and travel together, and who are clearly close to each other. The explanation has always expressed the requirement to give space to the honour of the junior man. Without his honour, he could no longer continue to serve.

The rhetorical bias which is so notable in Arabic, whether cause or effect, runs with a love of the extravagant, the shade side of Arabian asceticism. While this means that we have to remember to insert our own more turgid mentality's decimal point to the lavish comments which run so effortlessly in Arabic, we have also to watch out for other more unusual processes at work. Enter the 'optative aorist' and 'analogic thought' – recherché, but worth a brief mention because they encapsulate differences we sense, but find hard to analyse.

The 'optative aorist' is the use of the past tense to express a wish. This is found in ancient Greek, but not English. It is common in Arabic. The point is that declaring that something has already happened in a way makes it already a done fact. Thus, 'May God bless you' comes out in Arabic as 'God has blessed you.' There are connections here with the psychology of unbreakable oaths, curses, blessings and spells. The power of speech, representing other powers, like personality, spirit and knowledge, is thought, in many cultures, to effect real consequences. The thought that a good person sincerely uttering a blessing does actually invoke a divine grace is a beautiful one. But, for simple day-to-day purposes, this can also mean that the outsider listening to an account of arrangements, agreements or plans does well to stay alive to the difference between what has happened and what remains in the vaguer realm of desire. 'I have done it' may contain a wish or intention that I should be able to do it tomorrow. The fact that there are only two tenses in Arabic, past completed and present continuous (which is also used for the future), does not make this possible ambiguity any easier. The subject is only worth mentioning as an opportunity for easy mis-understanding and, on our side, the temptation we suffer to dismiss somebody as 'hopelessly unreliable'.

Similarly, the cautious codicil to many arrangements for the future, '*In Sha Allah*' ('If God has willed it'), may or may not be casually meant. Some still believe that the world in important senses is 'new every morning' and it would be an impiety to presume on the future. Behind this also lies a down-to-earth recognition of the pressure of obligations. Some of these, for instance hospitable attention to the guest in a society where 'doors' are notionally still kept open, like the sides of a tent, are absolute. A date outside with some foreigner just does not let the host off the hook, if a guest turns up just before he is due to leave home for the appointment. Family comes first and in enormous families there are always demands on one's time which cut across personal plans. As far as contact with foreigners is concerned, we are often frustrated. On the other side, Arabs confess that invitations are fraught with anxieties. 'Who else is going to be there? Will they bring their wives and will I look odd and conservative, if I don't bring mine? Would my wife be able to cope, anyway? Is the foreigner going to offer alcoholic drinks, will others accept them and shall I? What about guests who turn up after me?' In more tribal societies, the basic elements of a big dinner party given at home are likely to be a whole lamb and a pile of rice. A friend told me of his utter confusion when, at the home of an Englishman who was also his new boss, he was asked if wanted a slice cut off a leg of lamb, rare from the middle or well-done from the edge. So new was he to all this, he was even worried that he was being made the object of some humiliating practical joke. He admitted it had taken him a while to settle himself down again.

A sub-set of the same cast of mind is the notion that because one's cause is right and therefore just, if the cause is plainly articulated, then justice will prevail (and I shall get my own way). Argument is superfluous. One is reminded of the traditional opening of the naval rating when complaining to an officer, 'I wish to state a complaint, Sir.' The facts speak for themselves. Justice can only be done. The Palestinian cause has suffered a lot from over-reliance on this approach on one side and, on the other, from insensitivity to this mentality. Since the days before Islam to today's politics, this style of rhetorical appeal is familiar. We, of course, find it trying. It invites no argument, nor allows it. Its stridency can turn off sympathy. The splendour of the rhetorical presentation is usually lost in translation.

'Analogic thought' is not at all confined to the Arabs, but they are comfortable with it and remembering it helps us to look for the intended, but unspoken message, in a statement. We have always to work out what is going on, in what is happening. The anthropologist Mary Douglas unlocked this for me in her analysis of the Old Testament Book of Leviticus[5] where she distinguishes between

5 Douglas, Mary, *Leviticus As Literature* (Oxford, Oxford University Press, 1999), pp. 13–29.

analogic and dialogic thought as two thought styles which coexist and need each other, but offer very different possibilities for describing why things happen and what is happening. She touches on the work of Marcel Detienne who was interested in the difference between the 'magico-religious speech' of ancient Greek poetry and religion and the 'dialogue speech' we associate with Greek philosophy. He focuses on the experience of the 'hoplite revolution', the innovation of a professional army which brought together troops and officers from different regions. They had no dialect in common and so had to develop a new way of speaking to build up the army and be clear about operations. The result was 'dialogic thought' which moves in straight lines, incrementally building up the sense and argument, placing great emphasis on objective clarity. 'Analogic thought', in contrast, is the more instinctive human activity and it works on simile, metaphor and analogy from a shared resource of imagery and experience. This can make for a more vivid, sharp and entertaining diction, not necessarily an easy one. In small communities, the possibilities are great for the rapid coding of even haphazard but striking thoughts through allusions with which the listeners will connect. In early Arabic poetry, the use of extended metaphors, sometimes with internal dramas separate to the main theme, illustrate this thought style and its expression. Two things can happen at once. A careful construction of associations can build up one argument and simultaneously create a parallel implied argument which says something rather different. If this sounds complicated, we do it ourselves, though often perhaps subliminally.

In the Arab milieu, pressurized by the group and where everything is political because there are no politics, it makes for a sophistication of communication which is seriously complicated. A very crude illustration would be a learned magazine article by a member of the Muslim Brotherhood about the references in the Koran to the Pharaohs. This, on closer reflection, turns out to be a detailed critique of contemporary Egyptian government activities. Of course, not a direct word has been said. During the Cold War, there used to be jokes that specialists read the Soviet press with theodolytes to measure how the newspaper treated the news on the front page. In the Middle East, skills akin to the water diviner's are a help, if we want to detect the currents running beneath the surface.

Knowing that signals are important and can be misunderstood, Arabs give each other time to catch on. Years ago, if tribesmen in the deep sands of south-east Arabia saw other people in the desert and wanted a word with them, they would walk across, carefully kicking up sand with each step. I only saw this once. It indicated peaceful intentions, no shooting, please. At first meeting, the greetings and enquiries after health seem to us interminable. It is like listening to a fax handshake on a phone line. No apparent new information is exchanged, but impressions are being read and judgements made. Impatience to transmit can be impolite.

An occasion of this for me was a visit to Abu Dhabi and a meeting with Salim bin Ghubaishah who had travelled with Thesiger on his crossings of the Empty Quarter. Recently he had moved up from the sands to live in Abu Dhabi at the invitation of Shaikh Zayid. I sent him word that Wilfred had asked me to look him up. The British ambassador kindly said we might meet at his house and Salim and I had coffee and cakes in the drawing room. Salim must have been well into his seventies, but looked younger with his full beard, dyed bright orange with henna. He sat cross-legged on the sofa and with a placid but immobile face continued the formulas of greeting which had begun as he came into the room. At one point, he paused. I watched. Salim, holding my gaze, lifted his eyebrows to full elevation and then dropped them. No other change of expression. This enchanting gesture, I could only assume, was his variant for the wireless operator's 'How do you read me?' Involuntarily, I momentarily wrinkled my nose to pass the signal 'Roger', and then we carried on. We got Wilfred on the phone in England and Salim went through the greetings routine again. He finally told Wilfred he was planning to visit him and later in the summer indeed did so.

Arabs, like most people, love news and gossip. It helps locate people and reinforces the network. The greetings formulas include 'What's the news? Anything new?' But getting into the mode of a real exchange is not straightforward; and all the assurances of warmth, and the gentle compliments should not be taken at face value. A number of codes for trust have to be exchanged and verified first. The defences of suspicion and the anticipation of danger are not quickly dismantled. Public space is of its nature dangerous. It lies beyond the frontiers of family and blood; power has access; it is terrain which has to be navigated with care.

Coffee plays a key role as a symbol to ease these introductions. It also expresses the unity and diversity of the Arabs. At its most austere in Arabia, coffee is made with very lightly roasted beans, one part coffee and one part cardamom or occasionally clove which is very fierce. The person serving the coffee stays standing and pours a few drops into a small cup which he offers to the seated guest. The guest drinks this and can ask for more, but only twice more. When he wants no more, he shakes the cup lightly in his fingers as he hands it back. A guest is not entirely welcomed until this procedure is complete. Not serving coffee used to be tantamount to saying that a state of war existed between the two parties. The coffee cup has to be offered and taken in the right hand. More than a few drops in the cup can be carelessness in pouring, or something just short of an insult. I once saw a very dry-minded Arab take the cup, see that too much had been poured into it, turn the cup up to let the coffee fall onto the ground and hand it back empty with a shake and a stare at the coffee boy. Coffee is usually 'on the go' and the thermos has proved a great help, but a newly made coffee is required for serious guests. The coffee boy's musical, rhythmic grinding of the coffee with a wooden pestle and mortar (and each had his own music to make) was once an open invitation to any who could hear it, that they were welcome to join the company in receiving the guest.

What we would call 'Turkish coffee' (coffee with a heavy deposit of fine grounds in the bottom) is served as Arab coffee in many countries and as 'National Coffee' in Syria. Reading fortunes in the grounds in the bottom of the finished cup is a custom sometimes popular with women and taken surprisingly seriously by some of them, as is reading the palm of the hand. Coffee is a basic welcome gesture in Egypt and all across North Africa, though in Morocco mint tea sometimes takes over. Small glasses of sweet black tea follow coffee. Today sometimes a tray of coffee and tea is offered and no offence taken if the coffee is not chosen. Coffee served towards the natural end of a meeting or an evening is a sure sign that it is time to go. Each society regards the coffee ritual as its own, a local custom. There are, it is true, some small local variations, but the theme is uniform and an expression of the common attachment to hospitality as a value.

In language and other signals Arab culture has great sophistication and self-confidence. It is sensitive to the personal and yet draws the individual always towards the good of the group.

Chapter 10

Outlook

Fundamental questions arise when we look at the relationship between the individual and the collective. The Arab case, with its different dimensions of identity, is a hard one. Modern or traditional, tribal or urban, observant in religion or relaxed, political or apolitical, these labels each fit most individuals at some point or other. In the rapidly changing societies of the Middle East people look for bearings and direction, they explore new opportunities, return to what matters most to them and launch off again. Nothing is static and much is unpredictable, not least a surprising reliance on the past just as much as a surprising enthusiasm for what is new.

Blood, whether as household, family, tribe or genealogy, is under pressure from urbanization and globalization. Family concerns have to vie for time as the main talk with macro and societal problems and recurrent crises. Globalization may empower both the individual's choice and, even in limited circumstances, his access to knowledge. But it imposes burdens too: as he is included in the streams and cross-currents of a wider world, the individual feels a certain anonymity and powerlessness. He sees a 'me first' individualism at work in the West. He faces stiff competition in finding housing and work.[1] And so to survive, he may find that subconsciously his own attitudes have been gravitating towards such an outlook. The balance between the ancient individualism embedded in Arabian culture and the strong sense of the needs of the group can get disturbed. In the end, however, reliance on blood ties may

---

1 Statistics are drawn from the UNDP Report on Arab Human Development (2004). The report puts unemployment at 15 per cent and notes that each year there are roughly six million new entrants to the labour force across the region.

remain his ultimate security. And in order to network and beat the odds, he may find he has to use these ties and so he brings the conflict of contexts full circle.

Religion offers him a framework of values which he believes are of universal application. When he is abroad, being an Arab Muslim may be source of pride because, quite apart from having to face prejudices about terrorist associations, he does have the Arabic. At home, however, there are no longer any safe simplicities. Political and social tensions may cry out for solutions and his religion appears to offer them, but daily life imposes its own requirement for compromise and moderation. His loyalties and interests may be divided; his commitment hesitant. The strong resurgence of political Islam and today's friction between Sunnis and Shi'is provoke strong reactions, even atavistic ones, but also sketch out uncertainties for social, economic and political life for which the region seems quite unprepared. Language and knowledge present him with problems, lacking both the specialist understanding of the terms and context of religious debates and the personal educational formation to think critically about approaches to culturally new dilemmas.

Arab identity remains strong. In North Africa, it distinguishes the Arab from the African and European neighbours; in the Levant from the Israelis, Armenians, Circassians, Kurds and others; in Iraq too it marks him off from the minorities and, in addition, from the Iranians with their 70 millions. In the heartland of Arabia, other nationals (and many of these are not Arab) confront him on every side – they account for 25 per cent of the population in Saudi Arabia and two-thirds of the population in the other Gulf states. These were the figures given in 1990[2] and they are unlikely to have gone down since. Arab identity owns a grand past but today also a sense of unfulfilment and, for some, also perhaps a sense of shame, a feeling of being a victim in the face of the intractable problems of the region. The outsider is usually framed with being the author of these problems. The fact that Arab nationalist positions are now falling

2 See previous note.

out of vogue does not mean that he has lost a strong sense of community, or grievance against the foreigner.

Nationality has become, away from home, the label which defines the first meeting reactions of others, whether dislike, suspicion, affection or a gleam of self-interest. I cannot remember hearing a disobliging comment being made about the Bahrainis, Omanis or Tunisians; but whatever the justice of the rest of the banter, the prejudices and jokes have taken deep hold. They attach to individuals, and their natural counterpoint – pride in nationality – is part of today's outlook. This outlook, by our own measures, remains indissolubly gregarious.

These turning arguments about the self may seem unending, but they do not obliterate the aspiration to nurse high ambitions, achieve great honour and to make a difference. The sense that there is much to be done, is dynamic and multifaceted. The outsider's conventional agenda for the region is large: the reform of public services, defence expenditure and education in particular, and new investment in national infrastructure; defending human rights; promoting economic diversity and economic integration into the world economy; finding a solution to impending water shortages; planning the implications of population growth and the need to create employment; the stewardship of oil resources in a twitchy market and a carbon conscious world; finding a way ahead for the Palestinians and the Israelis; re-integrating Iraq into the community of the Gulf and a wider region; managing relations with Iran; internal security and the New Threats of terrorism, weapons of mass destruction and strategic crime. Under the heading of regime 'private business', we add the succession, constitutionality, the rule of law and the clamour about democracy. And throughout all the lists, the rights, freedoms and interests of women suffuse the agenda, like the colours in a piece of cloth.

The list of 'things to do' appears dismaying and is quickly taken as an affront to regional pride. Political sensitivities are set on a hair-trigger. The familiar riposte is that, having had a look at the Western world with its disintegrating family life, moral relativism, material selfishness and secularism, the Arab world should be left to find its own solutions. Respect for local culture is an enciphered phrase which conceals a defensive voice fearful for honour and fearful of a world which appears to have forgotten the meaning of it. The riposte also expresses a sense of shock that 'internal affairs' are no longer private or, indeed, sovereign. The outsiders' list, complete or not, is well meant, of course, and makes a good statement of our own pragmatic and utilitarian attitudes. And in this way, it tends to concentrate on incidentals, rather than fundamentals. For successful work on any of the 'to do' items would presuppose success in clarifying and reconciling the underlying ideas. One of these is accountability.

Accountability is to family, to cultural tradition, to religious law and to the face of power. The mismatch between the moral aspirations of the Arabs and their experience of power breaks the circuitry that makes accountability coherent. Corruption makes the point. Corruption is as plain as a wall to those who are not bene-fiting from it. In the family, it is teased into restraint. In the tribe, it denies the equality of individuals; and therefore the corrupt find their reputation diminished; this creates a general inhibition and encourages strong antibodies against corruption. In religion, the texts unambiguously condemn it. Public space is corruption's habitat and one reason for this is the near impossibility of calling it to account. The buck is passed. And who is to say if this is because power sees advantage in helping itself to the common good and buying off trouble, or because the idea of the common good is itself vague, when power is absolute? In this muddle, the mitigating excuses are legion. The culture of generosity needs funding; single resource economies are notoriously difficult to manage equitably and the 'trickle down' idea forces a need to meet yet greater demands for hand-outs; 'public money' is impersonal and therefore in practice more neutral than a friend's or relation's money ... and 'no one is paid enough anyway'. In the end, corruption sets in because people can get away with it. Its effects become another hard fact of life. Power's lack of accountability is at the heart of the problem. The common good just loses meaning when it is not held in common.

The absence of the common good, as a common experience and idea comprehensively applied, contributes to the dangers of the public space. This turns people in on themselves, to rely on their own networks. The *'wasitah'* system[3] is often misunderstood as being a manifestation of corruption. In itself *wasitah* is just networking. We often confuse it with *mahsubiyah,* which is favouritism and patronage. *Wasitah,* abused to gain unfair advantage, results in injustices and deplorable malfunctions. For much of the time, it just makes connections and communications possible which put people together as persons and not anonymous items. Like the *majlis* system, this is a hard school in human politics and those whose capital of contacts gives them prestige, have learned an enormous amount. They help themselves, but also the needy. The debate about it is unending, as it must be until accountability which reveals the quality of decisions and behaviour is upheld. Accountability should not stall as it goes uphill.

Outside the region, the analysis centres on political reform. The preferred diagnosis is to see a need to constrain power and therefore the instinct is to prescribe the house treatment, democracy. We believe in the devolution of power to prevent it being seized by catch-as-catch-can when a threat is felt or the chance of gain spotted. We hope to soften its sharper edges by engineering systems which wear it down and weigh it down. We view the street fight of politics with misgivings and so we delegate it to a self-selecting caste of politicians who are happy to join the fray and, we hope, do well for us in it. In the case of the English, with our historical record of institutionalized aggression, we are content to see the politicians using up some of their energy in party and parliamentary conflict. Parliamentary democracy has seen us well. By preserving our monarchies and instituting presidencies with limited terms, we are further able to contain power. We can protect ourselves from too much of a personalization of power. Personalization happens, but only for a human season. Overall, protected by the system of

3 Pronounced *'wasta'* – this is the system of mediation through friendly or obliged intermediaries.

elections, our requirements for accountability are satisfied. Secondary protections from the abuse of power, like the law, freedom of speech, the media, professional institutions and so on, are secured by this insistence that he who would assume power, has to answer for it. In the meantime, freed from the daily obligations of power, the rest of us can work away at our own callings.

This syndrome of content is readily recognized by Arabs. They applaud it, are amused by its magic coherence and wish us well with it. If it could be successfully transplanted, many would think that a fine thing. The obstacles, of course, are radical and of great value to them. The tradition, simply in the empirical sense, of absolute power took deep root a long time ago. Its story is violent and, for domestic purposes, the minatory capabilities of today's regimes are very large. The face of power does not blink. For leaders, honourable and honoured retirement at home is not on offer, save perhaps on occasions for the Lebanese.[4] Societies with long experience of absolute power, where the principles of personal equality and honour, of solidarity and the obligations of religion towards the group still have meaning, do not readily welcome the intrusion of power. Power is preferred at a distance where, indeed, it has traditionally resided. There are also structural issues.

The aggregation of family loyalties is tribe. In several of today's states, the regime is effectively defined by family or tribe. For the people, in the shadow of power, family and tribe remain the context for individual lives and are the strong elemental structures of society. 'Tribe' has a bad name because the tribes were given to a chivalry of violence, both in honour code and economic distribution, in the days before strong central government. The tribes stood for an (apparently) aristocratic opposition to modernization. Many tribal people lived in, or close to, poverty and were a rebuke or affront to the modernizing ambitions of the people of the towns. The tribes personified a hostility to the pretensions of nationalism when the

4 The shaikhs of the Trucial Coast, admittedly constrained in power since 1820 by their treaty relationship with Great Britain, are an interesting variation: they did agree in 1971 to concede some of their powers to their new federal structure, the United Arab Emirates.

new states were young. Tribal loyalties straddled the new borders. In fact, as we have seen in Iraq, the tribes' refusal to disappear, even after 40 years of socialism, and their ability to mobilize when political outcomes are uncertain, have shown a remarkable resilience. That fact also stubbornly sits on the plate as food for thought for regimes which have not yet been subjected to change.

The tribes' own failure, however, to think creatively about roles they might play in different political scenarios, has left them stranded. They have relied on their great competence in playing the current games, infiltrating and manipulating the status quo, rather than conceiving new agendas. In the past, they have also suffered from cultural inhibitions. They used not to promote the academic excellence which might have given them the prestige and techniques to be heard in wider fora and also abroad. Foreign languages have been in short supply. They appear to have missed the opportunities which might have once existed in Iraq. They did not make their number with the Americans, in spite of the extremely difficult cultural barriers they faced.

The conventional wisdom remains, with an almost arithmetical finality, that tribe into democracy 'won't go'. As a consequence, a social capital of values, experience and organization is marginalized. Or, more accurately, it operates subliminally. How tribes and families, the ineradicable internal geometry of many Arab societies, could be involved in ways of constraining power and allowing the people some sort of participation in its validation, remains an unanswered question. Not addressing this question will not remove the need to keep the tribal factor in mind in making practical political calculations.

Quite apart from the fact that they exist, a reason for looking at the tribes as a potential political utility is that they attach a high value to personal equality before the law and to individual freedom. They have preserved highly skilled traditions of consensus seeking and conflict resolution. Individual freedom and consensus through tolerance are not strongly apparent values characterizing the other main *political* trend which commands loyalty today, or the political groupings which affirm it, the political call to religion.

Investing religion with power also has a long tradition in the Middle East. Blood and family were major points of discord in the early days, as we have seen. In our own days, tribal social techniques have been of great value to Islamist groups, networking their way along the transnational routes of globalization. For many urban and urbanized people, the sense of belonging available in these 'neo-tribal' groups is a powerful comfort, providing, in purely emotional and social terms, what extended families and Sufi associations used to provide. In Arabia, in the early history of the caliphs, religion was a defence against the alien and over-mighty. Many tribes rallied to support the banner of the legitimacy of 'Ali and his successors in opposition to the increasingly Persian and Turkish tone at Baghdad. To say that these tribes were Shi'i at that time would be to oversimplify. The point is that the religion worked well as a language for disputing power. That seems to be also the case today.

The idiom of religion also had strong efficacy, not only as a means of harnessing tribal energy and honour, but also in composing tribal tension and conflict. Ernest Gellner, in his *Saints of the Atlas*,[5] describes a tribal world in Morocco where hereditary families of religious men lived, dedicated to providing judgements and conflict resolution for the surrounding tribes. The religious register here worked as a 'supra-tribal' medium in which fierce disputes, whether individual or collective, could change tack and find agreement. It was a remarkable example of how people find their own way to workable solutions, if power (in the Moroccan case, the tribal leaders) acknowledges constraints.

This technique, by design or serendipity, was part of Ibn Sa'ud's political success in dominating central Arabia in the eighteenth century. By his alliance with Muhammad Ibn 'Abd al-Wahhab, who was preaching a puritanical form of Hanbali Islam in Najd, he also created a supra-tribal model for military organization. In the twentieth century, during the resurgence of the family's power and establishment of the modern state, the same glue held. The prestige

5 Gellner, Ernest, *Saints of the Atlas* (London, Routledge Kegan & Paul, 1969).

of the descendants of Muhammad Ibn 'Abd al-Wahhab, known as
Al al-Shaikh (The Family of the Shaikh), was held in high regard for
more than two centuries and members of the family intermittently
had senior positions in the *'ulama* of the Saudi state. Ideologically,
this may have been a shared project between the two families, but
power remained with the sword, the Saudi family.

Religion thus offers both a language for political programmes (in
our terms) and, by the way, possibilities for managing personal, or
family, rule, but on a small scale. Some on the Islamist modernizing
wing see it as a way of dismantling the influence of the tribes. The
Iraqi situation remains too fluid to allow clear forecasting, but the
prospect of parties which are in fact confessional groupings seeking
to protect the interests of particular sects, lies ahead. Outsiders who
are not Muslims, have to wonder at the prospect of associating
power and religion in this way. The arguments from the past,
arguments about injustices which have occurred and which must be
prevented from reoccurring, are strong. The mere fact, however, of
elections, affecting though they may be when held after long dic-
tatorships, is not enough. More important still will be the answers to
the questions which must be asked about the structuring of power.
We are no strangers to politicians who hold their positions on the
vote of a small proportion of the electorate. The consequences bear
deeper thought. The encroachment on personal freedoms implicit in
some religious political manifestos raises serious worries for dis-
senters and many women.

Israel, a society which defines itself in ethnic and religious terms,
raises interesting and thematic analogies, but they are of limited
relevance. The Likud/Labour competition has traditionally dominated the scene. Even though both have been critically dependent on
religiously based parties to secure a coalition majority, their heritage
is well established and supported by many Israelis who are immigrants from societies long used to systems of political parties.
Secularism is a strong tradition. Israel has also had a particular and
unifying dynamic due to living in a state of hostility with its
neighbours for most of its existence. Nonetheless, the Arabs quickly
point out the sizable Arab minority's qualified access to welfare and

civil amenities. Ethnic and religious platforms are problematic for coherent democracy of the kind we know.

The question must remain open whether our practice of democracy is actually well suited to the region. The prescription of a party system for an Arab democracy must admit of a remarkable possibility. This is that parties will be able to compete equally, even those on electoral platforms which are religious in character, appealing to the population on creed and religious practice; and that a losing party of this type would be content to see its platform consigned to opposition, accepting that the electoral process is more important than their manifesto. This is way outside our own experience and, indeed, the Arabs'. The mainstream religious antipathy to *fitnah* (social discord and strife) is one major obstacle for a genuine adversarial party system and the wider culture of consensus which to a good extent derives from it, is another.

The Arab nationalist model for political development is of limited interest today, but, like a shadow in sunlight, inescapable. The states ruled by Arab nationalists were finding their way out of colonial or near-colonial mandate episodes. The nationalists themselves took over during a period of 'liberal experiment' which remains historically interesting, but it was not tested against sustained electoral competition. The outsiders were framed up as the external threat, responsible for all the troubles these people had seen. The founding of Israel, recognized as a foreign plantation, and the disaster of Suez greatly added to the Arab suspicion of outsiders' good faith and motives. This rhetoric, in whole or part, got into the idiom of Arab politics and is still emotive. It still snags apparently unrelated conversations. Analogical thought makes the connections ahead of us and we are all too often ambushed. The atmosphere of crisis in the 1950s was sympathetic to the emergence of unaccountable power centres. The casualty was mainstream political thinking which might have addressed the more basic ideas of politics and social justice. As a result, today, conversations on international politics are much livelier and better informed than talk about how internal politics might look.

The Arabs do complain of too much interference from outside.

They criticize our outsiders' inability to read subtleties, our commitment to regimes when they contingently suit our interests and our carelessness of consequences. They deprecate our mercantilism in selling hardware which reinforces hard power solutions to political problems, not least internally. They lampoon our shallow attitudes. Edward Said's *Orientalism*[6] won great applause in the region. A quiet comment made to me once was that the Arabs really just want to be left alone to sort themselves out, as suits them best. That perceptive advice catches the mood, but not the circumstances. The lights are turned on; the world watches because the region matters not only to its own people, but to the rest of us. The attempt to put us on the defensive often wins. They know our idiom better than we know theirs. The number of outsiders who have a working knowledge of Arabic and a personal depth of experience of the region, is tiny in comparison with its present significance to our own well-being. So we ourselves collude with the preferred arguments: we avoid domestic issues and stick to foreign affairs. We bring the ball back to our own goalmouth.

Many of the generalizations in this book would strike Middle Eastern readers as shallow and possibly unfair. If we had a more penetrating and discriminating knowledge of this part of the world, its peoples and their cast of mind, the motive for writing it would have been stilled. A massive effort is called for here to lift our own game. Had we had the knowledge, perhaps some of our mistakes would have been clearer in advance. Had we had the knowledge, perhaps our sympathies would have lent us insight and our judgements might have been surer.

The mood is sombre and only a superficial brio would put it otherwise. Nostalgia is part of the Arab jizz. In the high poetry of the desert, the pre-Islamic odes, a conventional beginning of a poem catches the poet pulling up his camel at the sight of the remaining traces of a camp – the burnt hearth stones, the scrapings in the earth and the collections of brushwood. He contemplates his emotions at the reminder of people he knew and their passing. He thinks of a

6 London, Routledge and Kegan Paul, 1978.

love that is gone and moves on to themes of solitude, fame and hard travel, the company he now keeps among the wildlife of the inner desert and its own unceasing drama of hunting, chase and death. He considers the days that were and the glory departed. Change and the hard indifference of time are the themes which Arabs applauded then and which have persuaded them to preserve this poetry through 15 centuries. It still finds its mark because pride in endurance and a stoical acceptance of the need to press on into the face of the fates are the food of those who know hardship.

In spite of this regretful attitude, the Arabs have enormous strengths on which to draw from their religion, social culture, their existential energy and intellectual heritage. They have a wealth of human capital; the jizz is powerful and has also this tension of potential. As they move away from the turbulence of the twentieth century, they may renew and innovate cultures and even institutions which secure what they value. They may find that they have what it takes to live confidently, meeting the challenges of living in a far wider world. Discontent, under-achievement and lack of confidence will cost us all dearly. In so far as integration brings us closer together, we should be clear how deeply held are their preferences and beliefs about family, religion and Arabism. Their own decisions about power, how to channel and constrain it, will greatly affect the success of our encounter.

Bibliography

Useful Reading

The proliferation of books and articles about the Arab world can leave the general reader bewildered. Listed below for readers' convenience are the books mentioned in the text and notes. The bibliographies in these books, especially Albert Hourani's and Robert Hoyland's (59 pages long), will be a safe guide for those wanting to read deeper into Arab history. Under 'Further Reading' are listed ten books which capture particular aspects of the Arab world and may be helpful.

Allen, Mark (1980) *Falconry in Arabia* (London, Orbis Publishing).

Blandford, Linda (1976) *Oil Sheikhs – In Quest of the New Arab* (London, Weidenfeld & Nicolson).

Bobbitt, Philip (2002) *The Shield of Achilles* (London, Penguin).

Douglas, Mary (1999) *Leviticus as Literature* (Oxford, Oxford University Press).

Douglas, Mary (2001) *In the Wilderness: The Doctrine of Defilement in the Book of Numbers* (Oxford, Oxford University Press).

Douglas, Mary (2004) *Jacob's Tears: The Priestly Work of Reconciliation* (Oxford, Oxford University Press).

Gellner, Ernest (1969) *Saints of the Atlas* (London, Routledge Kegan & Paul).

Haeri, Niloofar (2003) *Sacred Language Ordinary People* (New York, Palgrave Macmillan).

Halliday, Fred (1974) *Arabia Without Sultans* (London, Penguin).

Horne, Alastair (1978) *A Savage War of Peace* (London, Macmillan).

Hourani, Albert (1993) *A History of the Arab Peoples* (London, Faber).

Hourani, George (1971) *Islamic Rationalism – The Ethics of 'Abd al-Jabbar* (Oxford, Clarendon Press).

Hoyland, Robert (2001) *The Arabs and Arabia – From the Bronze Age to the Coming of Islam* (London, Routledge).

Kennedy, Hugh (2004) *The Court of the Caliphs* (London, Weidenfeld & Nicolson).

Lancaster, William and Fidelity (1992) 'Tribal Formations in the Arabian Peninsula', *Arabian Archaeology and Epigraphy*, 3, 142–72.

Lancaster, William and Fidelity (1999) *People, Land and Water in the Arab Middle East – Environments and Landscapes in the bilad ash-Sham* (Amsterdam, Harwood Academic Publishers).

Lancaster, William (1981) *The Rualla bedouin Today* (Cambridge, Cambridge University Press).

Lawrence, T. E. (1991) *Secret Despatches from Arabia and Other Writings*, ed. Malcom Brown (London, Bellew Publishing) – contains 'Twenty-Seven Articles' first printed in the *Arab Bulletin,* 20 August 1917.

Miles, Hugh (2005) '*al-Jazeerah – How Arab TV News Challenged the World*, (London, Abacus).

Mitchell, Richard (1969) *The Society of the Muslim Brothers* (Oxford, Oxford University Press).

Momen, Moojan (1985) *An Introduction to Shi'i Islam* (Oxford, George Ronald).

Pryce-Jones, David (1989) *The Closed Circle* (London, Weidenfeld & Nicolson).

Rayner, Steve (1982) 'The Perception of Time and Space in Egalitarian Sects: A Millenarian Cosmology', in *Essays in the Sociology of Perception* (London, Routledge and Kegan Paul).

Robertson Smith, William (1889) *The Religion of the Semites* (London).

Said, Edward (1978) *Orientalism* (London, Routledge and Kegan Paul).

Sakr, Naomi (2001) *Satellite Realms* (London, I. B. Tauris).

Scruton, Roger (2003) *The West and the Rest* (London, Continuum).

Shaban, M. A. (1971) *Islamic History AD 600–750 – A New Interpretation*, (Cambridge, Cambridge University Press).

United Nations Development Programme (2002, 2003, 2004) Regional Bureau for Arab States, *Arab Human Development Report* (New York).

Further Reading

Ajami, Fuad (1999) *The Dream Palace of the Arabs – A Generation's Odyssey* (New York, Vintage Books).

Arberry, Arthur J. (1964) *The Koran Interpreted* (Oxford, Oxford University Press – *The World's Classics*).

Bibliography

Al-Khalil, Samir (Kanan Makiya) (1993) *Cruelty and Silence – War, Tyranny, Uprising and the Arab World* (New York, W. W. Norton).

Batatu, Hanna (1978) *The Old Social Classes and the Revolutionary Movements of Iraq – A Study of Iraq's Old Landed and Commericial Classes and of its Communists, Ba'thists and Free Officers* (Princeton University Press).

Dam, Nikolaos van (1979) *The Struggle for Power in Syria – Sectarianism, Regionalism and Tribalism in Politics, 1961–78* (London, Croom Helm).

Dam, Nikolaos van (1996) *The Struggle for Power in Syria – Politics and Society under Asad and the Ba'th Party* (London, I. B. Tauris).

Kurpershoek, Marcel (2001) *Arabia of the bedouins* (London, Saqi Books).

Macmillan, Margaret (2001) *Peacemakers – The Paris Conference of 1919 and Its Attempt to End War* (London, John Murray).

Ruthven, Malise (2002) *A Fury for God* (London, Granta Books).

Sivan, Emmanuel (1985, reprinted enlarged edition 1990) *Radical Islam – Medieval Theology and Modern Politics* (Yale University Press).